Clustering
Standards in
Integrated
Units

Second Edition

Clustering
Standards in
Integrated
Units

Second Edition

Diane L. Ronis

CORWIN PRESS
A SAGE Publications Company
Thousand Oaks, CA 91320

For information:

Corwin Press
A Sage Publications Company
2455 Teller Road
Thousand Oaks, California 91320
www.corwinpress.com

Sage Publications India Pvt. Ltd.
B 1/I 1 Mohan Cooperative Industrial Area
Mathura Road, New Delhi 110 044
India

Sage Publications Ltd.
1 Oliver's Yard
55 City Road
London EC1Y 1SP
United Kingdom

Sage Publications Asia-Pacific Pte. Ltd.
33 Pekin Street #02-01
Far East Square
Singapore 048763

Printed in the United States of America

Library of Congress Cataloging-in-Publication Data

Ronis, Diane L.
Clustering standards in integrated units / Diane L. Ronis.—2nd ed.
     p. cm.
Includes bibliographical references and index.
ISBN 978-1-4129-5556-0 (cloth)—ISBN 978-1-4129-5557-7 (pbk.)
1. Education—Standards—United States. 2. Curriculum planning—United States. I. Title.

LB3060.83.R66 2008
379.1′580973—dc22   2007011196

This book is printed on acid-free paper.

07   08   09   10   11   10   9   8   7   6   5   4   3   2   1

Acquisitions Editor:	Hudson Perigo
Editorial Assistant:	Jordan Barbakow
Production Editor:	Astrid Virding
Copy Editor:	Pam Suwinsky
Typesetter:	C & M Digitals (P) Ltd.
Proofreader:	Andrea Martin
Indexer:	Molly Hall
Cover Designer:	Monique Hahn

Contents

Preface   vii

    Why Johnny Can't Read—or, for That Matter,

        Write, Multiply, or Divide   vii

Introduction   xi

    Moving From Convention to Constructivism   xi

    The Case for Planning With Units   xii

    How to Use This Book   xiii

Acknowledgments   xv

About the Author   xvii

1. **Unit Components: Tools for Building Units**   1

    The Evolution of Knowledge and the Need

        for Planning With Units   1

    Standards: What's the Big Idea?   1

    Addressing Standards Using Integrated Instruction   2

    Using the Culminating Task Organizer   3

    Designing the Culminating Task Rubric:

        The Key to Successful Planning   5

    Using the Unit Planning Map and the Unit Overview   6

    Lesson Planning in the Context of Unit Design   6

    Creating the Most Effective Integrated Unit Plan   10

    Sample Units   11

2. **Organizing Instruction for Meaning:**

   Planning for Learning and Achievement   23

    Making Learning Meaningful   23

    Working With How the Brain Works   23

    Comprehensive Design   25

    Performance Tasks and Products   25

    Culminating Task Organizer   27

    Valuing Content and Student Perspective   28

    Sample Units   29

3. How to Build a Better Rubric: Developing a Unit Assessment Plan   **39**

Performance Assessment   39

Rubrics to the Rescue   40

Progress Assessment Rubric   42

Designing Rubrics With and for Students   44

Sample Units   52

4. Unit Panorama: Using the Unit Planning Map and the Unit Overview   **67**

Bringing the Big Picture Into Focus   67

Unit Design: Addressing the Many Facets of Meaning   67

Curricular Models   68

Choosing Which Tool to Use   70

Planning for Success   73

Sample Unit   78

5. The Interdisciplinary Lesson Plan: Facilitating Investigation   **93**

A Lesson Well Learned   93

Approaching Content   93

Best-Laid Plans   95

An Environment That Inspires Learning   95

Sample Unit   96

Appendix I: Content Area Standards   **103**

Online State Content Standards   103

Professional Organizations' Web Sites Related to Standards   104

Standards and the Nature of School Mathematics:

    National Council of Teachers of Mathematics   105

The National Science Education Standards   110

International Society for Technology in Education   110

Language Arts, the NCTE/IRA, and Problem-Based Learning   116

Standards for the Social Studies   118

The Visual Arts   118

Appendix II: Planning Forms   **123**

Culminating Task Organizer   124

Rubric Organizer   125

Rubric for Problem-Based Instruction   126

Rubric for Accelerated Problem-Based Instruction   127

Unit Planning Map   128

Unit Overview   129

Interdisciplinary Lesson Plan   130

Teacher's Unit Plan Self-Evaluation Rubric   131

Bibliography   **133**

Index   **139**

Preface

WHY JOHNNY CAN'T READ—OR, FOR THAT MATTER, WRITE, MULTIPLY, OR DIVIDE

The challenging road to educational improvement is full of twists and turns. Many questions arise as to where we are going and why we are going there in the first place. Because of how our society has recently evolved, an educational paradigm shift has become vital. Commerce now functions in a global arena filled with fierce international competition, while technology has become an essential part of our daily lives. For educators, the present set of continually shifting circumstances can often be confusing. While daily discoveries about the brain are revolutionizing the ways in which we view learning, cyberspace and the Internet are revolutionizing the ways in which we view instruction. In spite of the anticipation and innovation accompanying this fluid state of affairs, our current educational system remains as unchanged as it has been for the past 150 years. This production-line model sees children as raw materials that, when uniformly treated in an identical manner (under closely controlled and monitored conditions), will result in an educated population.

Schools are continually being modified and changed; however, this has always been done with the aim of making them more efficient rather than more compassionate. It is for this reason that all centralized education reforms focus on tests and accountability. Politicians and administrators interested in costs and results continually try to make the current system work better rather than analyze whether or not the system works.

In our race to be the best, we have forgotten what schools are for and how people learn. The old idea (which we seem to take for granted) is that people learn from experience. Everything a person does throughout his or her life leaves a mark upon that individual. Contrary to the experience model, however, the idea currently dominating education and business posits that people learn through the acquisition of information.

The failing of this information acquisition approach is that rote learning of isolated facts is the most difficult way for our brains to learn and the most common reason we forget. Simply learning facts is no guarantee of knowledge or wisdom. Drills do not help children learn reading, writing, mathematics, or, for that matter, anything else, unless there is an underlying comprehension (which, of course, makes the drill unnecessary to begin with).

Experience is how we acquire almost all of our learning, both the desirable and the undesirable. What many students experience in school today, however, is failure. What they need to experience instead is productive success. Today's learner bears little resemblance to the student of the 1950s, 1960s, or 1970s. The family unit has undergone a drastic metamorphosis. Politicians talk about accountability and successful schools, yet no one talks about development of the successful child. How did we get to this sorry state of affairs?

The intergenerational stability of American traditions, values, and mores has been on the decline for many years, replaced by more egocentric beliefs. What we are witnessing is the evolution of a philosophy of self-gratification, personal satisfaction, and entitlement that has become an outcome of our harried and economically motivated lifestyles. It is electronic communication's vastly different viewpoints rather than the family that currently exert the most powerful socializing force in American culture. Social service agencies experience an increase in people requiring personal assistance to manage their lives on a daily basis.

Whether we want to admit it or not, there is an increasing percentage of students being reared in families with less stable and responsible parenting. Blended and alternative families are increasing rapidly, creating uniquely different child-rearing strategies, especially with regard to discipline. The result of these differing strategies is a declining respect for adult authority, the institution of schools, and the value of public education. The concepts of delaying gratification, commitments to long-term goals, and the pursuit of excellence have diminished, especially for the academically challenged. Social popularity and interpersonal interests dominate student school focus, creating an imbalance between the peer pressure/academic excellence dichotomy.

Today, student diversity is the norm for many districts, resulting in greater heterogeneous programming while homogeneous education declines. Numerous roles and obligations are assigned to school personnel, including a clinical-parenting responsibility to address whole child issues. Parent-school interactions have become increasingly litigious and confrontational, while public advocacy of school funding and management are continually challenged by local municipalities seeking greater input and accountability.

Educating this generation of learners is significantly more complex and personally demanding than in previous times and requires an entirely different educational philosophy with its own repertoire of interventions for success. To effectively educate this generation of learners, teachers need a multiplicity of tools, only one of which is the content knowledge that they bring to the classroom. In addition to such content knowledge, educators need to understand the scientific basis for how learning occurs. They need to be well versed in not only what neuroscientists have learned about the brain but also how to apply that learning to a classroom with 30 unique brains, each having its own learning style, array of abilities, intelligences, and challenges.

Testing, retesting, and then more testing will not help a generation of children learn to succeed in this complex and constantly changing world. The testing frenzy that has come into vogue this past decade has served only to move education further away from the connections and relevancy that make learning meaningful. It is as if the very remedy being sought is exacerbating the original malady. Instead of making the learning experience one that is meaningful to the student, curricula have become test driven and, therefore, more narrow. What educators are being forced to do at this juncture in time is prepare students to become test takers rather than critical thinkers.

For our youth to learn how to think and reason,

For them to be able to problem solve in new and unfamiliar situations,

To develop a generation of workers who can understand the dynamics of collaboration and synergy . . .

We need . . .

A curriculum that can teach these skills, a curriculum that not only is based on the understanding of the concepts underlying the content but also develops critical thinking by using the information we have available on how and when learning is most likely to occur . . .

A curriculum that frames a collective outlook of what quality education looks like in the twenty-first century and that can prepare the youth of America to become critical thinkers, problem solvers, and collaborators ready to take their places in a global society . . .

A curriculum that ignites curiosity and promotes lifelong learning . . .

An inquiry-driven, brain-compatible framework that can set as well as achieve rigorous standards . . .

A quality learning experience for all of America's children.

Introduction

MOVING FROM CONVENTION TO CONSTRUCTIVISM

The conventional way of teaching the subject disciplines has been to isolate each of them from their naturally integrated contexts and present them to learners as independent and discrete units. Unfortunately, this traditional format operates in opposition to the brain's intrinsically integrative processing of information. In mathematics classes, for example, information has been taken out of any kind of relevant context and is instead taught through the use of examples showing students how to solve problems and then having the students complete large numbers of similar problems (Battista, 1999). This process overlooks current research showing the following (O'Brien, 1999; Ronis, 2007b):

- Students develop knowledge through interaction between the student and the knowledge (active learning).
- Students do not think like adults.
- Students learn extremely well through social interaction.

The fact of the matter is that when young learners are enthusiastic about a fact or a concept that they have discovered, they are better able to retain this new information and use it in creative and meaningful ways. This essentially constructivist approach to learning posits that people learn best by doing rather than by listening alone. Such problem-based learning (sometimes referred to as "the project approach") involves a sustained, in-depth exploration of events, circumstances, or objects in the students' environment. These explorations are carried out in a way that encourages learners to raise questions and search for answers about topics that hold their interest. This inquiry model is based on the idea that knowledge is best acquired through the investigation and resolution of challenges and/or problems. The model presents students with relevant, integrated, and contextual issues—the same kinds of issues professionals deal with on a daily basis. Through the resolution of these integrated authentic problem situations, students develop and refine their abilities as self-motivated learners.

Since integrated, problem-based instructional methods are student centered rather than teacher centered (and problem based rather than solution based), they differ from more traditional instruction. In the traditional, subject-specific, teacher-oriented approach, it is the teacher who poses the problem and also supplies the information to the students. With the integrated, problem-based, inductive format, however, the teacher gives the students information but then asks the students to develop those questions that must be answered before they can proceed toward a resolution. With this second approach, it is the students who are the active participants in the process rather than the teacher, who is merely the facilitator. For the learning to be meaningful, a proffered problem must be realistic, relevant, and authentic (real world) so that students can relate to the problem's context. (For learners to become meaningfully engaged in problem-solving activities, they need to see the purpose behind the work to be done and understand its relevancy.)

With the use of authentic, real-world problems, students assume the roles of working professionals. The kinds of problems students will tackle are interdisciplinary, open-ended, and messy, and they contain only enough information to suggest how the learner might proceed with the inquiry, but never enough information to enable him or her to solve the problem without more in-depth investigation. Students must use such critical thinking skills as comparing and contrasting; the identification of similarities and differences; classification and sequencing; drawing analogies; strategy planning; drawing inferences and predicting outcomes; determining cause and effect; deductive and inductive reasoning; and logic, analysis, evaluation, synthesis, and interpretation.

Open-ended complex problems continue to evolve and become more complex as more information is gathered, usually concluding with an array of viable solutions. With such problems, it is the student-directed inquiry that drives the problem-solving process. When students grapple with the intricacies of these kinds of problems, they begin to discover what it is that they will need to know to arrive at an acceptable solution. Once in possession of this knowledge, they can then determine how to find and locate the information they will need. In this quest for knowledge and search for solutions, students become effective and self-directed problem solvers as well as collaborative team players.

A philosophical shift in which the focus moves from a teacher-centered perspective to a more student-oriented approach would foster a change from the management of an environment of conformity to the cultivation of an atmosphere of creativity. The teacher's role would shift from presiding over rows of isolated, front-facing students to facilitating small collaborative teams of students who face each other. No longer directing students to collect data on arbitrary topics, the teacher is free to encourage learners to investigate questions of direct relevance to their own lives. Thus, they move from repetitive drills and memorization of soon-to-be-forgotten information fragments to the synthesis and creation of new ideas. All of the aforementioned skills, attitudes, and abilities are what our children will need for success in this twenty-first century.

THE CASE FOR PLANNING WITH UNITS

Interdisciplinary unit planning allows teachers to teach outside the bounds of content area but requires that teachers demonstrate knowledge of content. It recognizes that students have a varied approach to learning and personally contextualize material. This approach enables students to make connections to the wider world and to their own experience.

HOW TO USE THIS BOOK

The ability to plan and prepare for instruction is a key component of professional practice (Danielson, 1996). Acknowledging this, *Clustering Standards in Integrated Units* presents frameworks and other instruments to aid both seasoned and novice teacher professionals in designing interdisciplinary instruction by doing the following:

- Developing learning activities that are aligned with instructional goals and standards
- Selecting appropriate instructional materials and resources that spark interest and facilitate individual connections that, in turn, promote meaning and understanding
- Evaluating student performance using an instrument that recognizes students' varied approaches to learning, knowledge bases, and cultural and language backgrounds while maintaining high expectations for all

Chapter 1—Unit Components: Tools for Building Units details the tools needed to effectively plan for and implement units that integrate content across multiple curriculum areas. Integrating content allows multiple standards to be clustered or addressed simultaneously. The tools presented include the Culminating Task Organizer, Culminating Task Rubric, the Unit Planning Map, the Unit Overview, and the Interdisciplinary Lesson Plan. Rubrics that feature the specific qualities of a well-constructed unit are offered so readers can evaluate the unit plans they develop using the templates and samples as guides.

Chapter 2—Organizing Instruction for Meaning: Planning for Learning and Achievement tackles the way in which instruction is made meaningful through the use of new information learned about the brain, including the positive roles emotions and social interactions play in the learning process. The construction of a quality Culminating Task is demystified through the use and explanation of the Culminating Task template. The chapter takes the reader through the process step by step, providing a checklist and guiding questions.

Chapter 3—How to Build a Better Rubric: Developing a Unit Assessment Plan makes the case for using rubrics as reliable scoring guides for student performance. A practical design methodology, which employs a difficulty multiplier (DM), is discussed. The DM takes into account individual differences among learners while applying an equitable means for evaluating the quality of individual performances. A number of rubrics are submitted as examples of how they can be used as part of an overall unit assessment plan.

Chapter 4—Unit Panorama: Using the Unit Planning Map and the Unit Overview presents the means for bringing the unit's big picture into focus. The Unit Planning Map and the Unit Overview are offered as the implements for organizing the many considerations inherent in unit planning. In addition, this chapter outlines curricular models and how they relate to unit design.

Chapter 5—The Interdisciplinary Lesson Plan: Facilitating Investigation focuses on the lesson's role in unit design. Lesson plans are the acknowledged underpinnings of successful instruction but are not the only factor that predicts or adds up to success. The parts that pedagogy and the instructional environment play are also explored.

Fully developed sample units conclude each chapter.

Appendix I features standards documents from several professional sources. Web sites for each state are listed, where more information can be obtained regarding respective state standards.

Appendix II contains blank templates in the form of blackline masters for each of the planning instruments presented.

A comprehensive bibliography concludes the book.

Acknowledgments

I would like to thank my student-colleagues for the time, effort, support, and inspiration that they contributed toward the realization of this dream:

Silas Meredith, Krista Emantrudo, Lauren Napier, Christine Torino, Dania Champlin, Julie Esposito, Anne Berndtson, Dave Brackett, Dean Bruenn, Mark Goldsmith, Brendan Lynch, Tim Shortt, Kristen Hines, Elizabeth Naves, Michele Flynn, Barbara Averna, Janetta Dobler, Patti Schumacher, Nancy Wengefeld, Mary Dunn, Brian Wind, Teri Scatamacchia, Amy Brown, Cyndi Barone, Michele Goode, Trisha Cassella, Eileen C. Warner, Erin Carath, Lisa DePino, Michelle Avallone, Jacqui Nelson, Chris Kalafus, Tara Moriarity, Anne Marrinan, Christopher Elgee, Kevin Reddy, Bernadette Riordan, Laurine Murray Post, and Irene Petrucci.

—Diane Ronis

Corwin Press gratefully acknowledges the following reviewers:

Nancy Betler, NBCT
Talent Development Program
Charlotte Mecklenburg Schools
Charlotte, NC

Marguerita K. DeSander
Assistant Professor, Leadership and Policy Studies
The George Washington University
Washington, DC

Launa Ellison
Educational Consultant
Minneapolis, MN

Joen M. Painter
Consultant
Jotihealth
Yuma, AZ

About the Author

Diane Ronis is currently a professor of education at Southern Connecticut State University and holds a PhD in curriculum and instruction. She has been involved in the field of education since 1968 and has been a keynote speaker and presenter at numerous conferences and workshops throughout the United States. Her area of expertise is in the transferring of neuroscientific research into practical strategies that classroom teachers can easily implement.

As a new professor in 1998, she began creating material for her classes that would be in keeping with her vision for cutting-edge, high-quality instruction and assessment methodologies that teachers would find easy to understand and implement. These materials evolved into the five books she has published: *Clustering Standards in Integrated Units, Critical Thinking in Math, Problem-Based Learning for Math and Science: Integrating Inquiry and the Internet, Brain-Compatible Assessments,* and *Brain-Compatible Mathematics.*

Unit Components

Tools for Building Units

THE EVOLUTION OF KNOWLEDGE
AND THE NEED FOR PLANNING WITH UNITS

Information and knowledge are growing far more rapidly than ever before. As Nobel laureate Herbert Simon stated, the meaning of "knowing" has shifted from being able to remember and repeat information to being able to find and use it (Simon, 1996). More than ever, the sheer magnitude of our expanding knowledge base makes coverage by a traditional education design impossible. Knowledge is not simply a list of facts and formulas that are relevant to a particular area of interest. Rather, knowledge is organized around core concepts or big ideas that guide thinking (National Research Council, 2002).

Professional organizations as well as local education agencies have sought to codify the big ideas in the form of standards.

STANDARDS: WHAT'S THE BIG IDEA?

When viewed as a creative challenge, the current standards movement has the potential to motivate educators and students to reach higher levels of performance. The movement offers a coherent vision for the future, defining excellence for performance standards as well as content standards in the various subject areas.

High-quality, standards-based instruction is a way for educators to shape the direction of change in American education. Standards provide an intelligent framework for curriculum when they are based upon sound educational principles. Whether they are put forth by professional associations or individual states, these standards can only help to raise the quality and caliber of education in the United States. The challenge in all of this will be to remain patient. It takes time for healthy change to be sustained and ultimately to achieve success. Quality standards, when put in place, serve only to strengthen the teaching profession.

The standards designed by the National Council of Teachers of Mathematics (NCTM), the National Council of Teachers of English (NCTE), the International Reading Association (IRA), the National Council for the Social Studies (NCSS), the National Academy of Sciences (NAS), and the International Society for Technology in Education (ISTE) are all based on sound research regarding the manner in which learning occurs. (See Appendix I: Content Area Standards for lists of these standards.)

Standards-based instructional policies are essential for the evolution and advancement of our current education system. Such policies can improve learning only if they are directly tied to efforts that increase the abilities of teachers and administrators to improve instruction (National Research Council, 2002). The most effective way to do this is by linking brain-compatible instruction and assessment methodologies with those standards systems and then implementing the systems in a way that provides coherent curricula for administrators, teachers, parents, and students. Teaching from integrated units is a readily usable means for accomplishing just that.

QUESTIONS TO ASK AT THE OUTSET OF UNIT PLANNING

- How will students use the skills and knowledge that scientists, engineers, designers, and others use in completing this performance task or product?
- How will this task or product relate to the developmental needs and interests of students?
- What are the specific qualities and characteristics that must be contained in the evidence of learning?
- What specific ways of documenting production, perception, and reflection will be used?

ADDRESSING STANDARDS USING INTEGRATED INSTRUCTION

In classrooms that incorporate both a standards-based teaching philosophy and a coherent vision of curriculum, students can use inquiry learning and problem solving to utilize and expand upon knowledge they already possess. They are able to apply that new learning to real-world problems and develop their own strategies to resolve even more complex issues. They interact with one another through the use of multiple and varied resources. Within this standards paradigm, teachers still teach, but their role is refocused: they now carry out instruction through the formation of problems that ask students to research, analyze, and synthesize new information while building upon the knowledge they already possess.

Integrated unit design arranges the learning so that it will be connected, contextual, and organized around important concepts (big ideas) that support understanding and the transfer of knowledge. By employing a unit plan, teachers are able to diagram the content of a unit prior to instruction. By addressing the quality and depth of the learning that will take place, teachers can ascertain ahead of time that instruction will be of the highest quality, productive, and enjoyable. Because this learning is relevant, contextual, and meaningful to students, their brains readily process it. Thus, what is learned becomes enduring knowledge rather than isolated bits and pieces of information that are memorized and soon forgotten. Figure 1.1 lists the tools for creating an integrated unit plan that are introduced in this chapter.

Figure 1.1   Tools for Creating the Integrated Unit Plan

✓   The Culminating Task Organizer
✓   Culminating Task Rubric
✓   The Unit Planning Map or the Unit Overview
✓   Lesson Model

USING THE CULMINATING TASK ORGANIZER

The integrated unit plan provides a framework that helps the educator reflect upon and organize change and development within the unit. When developing integrated inquiry units, the teacher will often find it best to begin with the design of the Culminating Task. The logic of this backward design format is to first create the activity or project (the evidence of learning), identify exactly which standards and/or results are being addressed, and then choose the content (specific lessons) to be taught so that students are prepared for successful completion of the Culminating Task. The Culminating Task helps to focus both student interest and teacher objectives through the choice of performance tasks that students will complete to exhibit evidence of learning (demonstration of their mastery of the content and processes used).

> **CHARACTERISTICS OF AN EFFECTIVE CULMINATING TASK**
>
> - Meaningful
> - Has application or connection to the real world
> - Has a high level of relevancy to students

Culminating Task Organizer Template

The Culminating Task is the hook that engages the students. A task must be meaningful, have application or connection to the real world, and have a level of relevancy that piques learner curiosity.

The Culminating Task provides the motivation to learn and sparks the desire to search for answers. Samples of completed Culminating Task Organizers can be found at the end of each chapter in this book.

TEMPLATE FOR CULMINATING TASK ORGANIZER

CURRICULUM AREA(S):

GRADE LEVEL(S):

PROJECT DURATION: *The essential information on which a Culminating Task is built*

RESOURCES/MATERIALS: *The practical needs (for example, construction paper, glue, performance space, tech lab time, 26 copies of* The Taming of the Shrew*)*

TASK/PROJECT DESCRIPTION

- *Details the task or activity that students will perform*
- *Guides students and gives them direction on the task parameters and how the work will be carried out*

STANDARDS ADDRESSED

Refers to the specific district, state, or national standards that underlie a quality curriculum

LANGUAGE ARTS	TECHNOLOGY
List of language arts content standards and process skills addressed by this project/activity	*List of technology content standards and process skills addressed by this project/activity*
MATHEMATICS	**SCIENCE**
List of math content standards and process skills addressed by this project/activity	*List of science content standards and process skills addressed by this project/activity*
SOCIAL STUDIES	**VISUAL ARTS**
List of social studies content standards and process skills addressed by this project/activity	*List of visual arts content standards and process skills addressed by this project/activity*

TASK/PROJECT OBJECTIVES

COMPREHENSION OF CONCEPTS	SKILL AND PROCESS DEVELOPMENT
Concepts that make up the learning objectives	*Skills or processes needed for the conceptual learning to take place*

PRODUCTS AND/OR PERFORMANCES

Describes the work that will be completed by students as a group as well as individually (This is a good place to use links to other curriculum areas.)

GROUP PRODUCTS	INDIVIDUAL PRODUCTS	EXTENSIONS
List of the product(s) created by the group	*List of the product(s) created by the individual group members*	*Ideas for students who wish to go beyond the requirements of the basic project*

CRITERIA FOR TASK/PROJECT EVALUATION

Create a criteria checklist for each group and/or individual product. These criteria checklists develop into the project rubrics.

GROUP PRODUCTS	INDIVIDUAL PRODUCTS	EXTENSIONS
Criteria checklist for group product(s)	*Criteria checklist for individual product(s)*	*Criteria checklist for extension activities*

DESIGNING THE CULMINATING TASK RUBRIC: THE KEY TO SUCCESSFUL PLANNING

The term *rubric* refers to an established set of criteria used for scoring or rating student work. A scoring rubric describes the levels of performance a student might be expected to attain relative to a desired standard of achievement. These performance descriptors tell the evaluator specifically which characteristics or indicators to look for in a student's work and then where to place that work on a predetermined scale or continuum.

Rubrics provide the means of communicating standards since they have the advantage of offering both students and parents the opportunity to understand what learning is taking place in the classroom as well as the content standards included in that learning. Introducing evaluation rubrics at the beginning of a study unit ensures that the student knows from the outset exactly what the teacher's expectations are for achievement. There are no surprises about the level of those expectations or how those expectations will be evaluated. Rubrics can be created and applied to all types of student work, including journals, portfolios, and performances.

Chapter 3 is devoted to the creation of rubrics to assess each facet of the unit.

TEMPLATE FOR RUBRIC				
	Performance descriptors			
Criteria Evaluated *Specific aspects of student work to be evaluated*	**1** **Novice** Beginning **No, Not Yet**	**2** **Basic** Developing **Yes, But**	**3** **Proficient** Accomplished **Yes**	**4** **Advanced** Exemplary **Yes Plus**
Criterion #1	*Description of quality at the beginning level*	*Description of quality at the developing level*	*Description of quality at the accomplished level*	*Description of quality at the exemplary level*
Criterion #2	Describes what student work will look like at each of the performance levels			
	Description of quality at the beginning level	*Description of quality at the developing level*	*Description of quality at the accomplished level*	*Description of quality at the exemplary level*
Criterion #3	*Description of quality at the beginning level*	*Description of quality at the developing level*	*Description of quality at the accomplished level*	*Description of quality at the exemplary level*
Criterion #4	*Description of quality at the beginning level*	*Description of quality at the developing level*	*Description of quality at the accomplished level*	*Description of quality at the exemplary level*

USING THE UNIT PLANNING
MAP AND THE UNIT OVERVIEW

The purpose of the Unit Planning Map or the Unit Overview is to provide the unit designer with a comprehensive perspective of the completed unit. When designing an integrated unit, the instructor uses either a Unit Planning Map or a Unit Overview. The Unit Planning Map is designed for the new or novice teacher, while the Unit Overview is better suited to a more seasoned teacher who consistently evidences "best practice" pedagogy. Using either tool, the unit designer can clearly see the rhythm and flow of the lessons (that is, the sequencing and integration of new information with information already known and understood). This is essential for meaningful learning to take place, because new ideas and information must be connected to previously learned concepts within a meaningful context for transfer to occur.

The Unit Planning Map is an analytical framework aid for the novice teacher. It serves as a graphic organizer for effective unit design and development so that the less experienced educator is able to plan well-integrated units of advanced quality. The Unit Planning Map includes those Lesson Perspectives omitted in the Unit Overview.

A sample of a completed Unit Planning Map can be found at the end of this chapter.

The Unit Overview is a complete framework that the experienced teacher can use to develop an effective and innovative integrated unit. Because pedagogy tends to be more highly developed in experienced teachers, the Unit Overview omits the Lesson Perspectives that are included in the Unit Planning Map.

A sample of a completed Unit Overview can be found at the end of Chapter 3.

LESSON PLANNING
IN THE CONTEXT OF UNIT DESIGN

The final stage of unit development is to identify the specific learning that needs to take place so that the Culminating Task can be successfully implemented. The following questions can serve to identify the specific instruction that will be needed:

- What content knowledge will students need to complete the task?
- What do students need to do to learn the content?
- What resources will you (the teacher) use?
- In what ways are these lessons related to students' interests?
- In what ways are they related to students' needs?
- What are the questions that need to be asked?

Chapter 5 more fully explores how to design meaningful and creative lesson plans as part of integrated units. A sample of a completed Interdisciplinary Lesson Plan appears at the end of Chapter 5.

TEMPLATE FOR UNIT PLANNING MAP		
UNIT AT A GLANCE *Foundation of the unit*	**LESSON 1**	**LESSON 1 PERSPECTIVE**
TOPIC: CURRICULUM AREA(S): GRADE LEVEL(S): PROJECT DURATION: UNIT OBJECTIVES: *Targets the unit's main purpose* TECHNOLOGY: *Innovative ways technology can be used to enhance student understanding and stimulate interest* ASSESSMENT: • *Means and opportunity for students to "show what they know"* • *Criteria for excellence known to all parties before undertaking an activity, task, or lesson* • *Select and use a variety of assessment techniques (for example, if process, problem-solving, and higher cognitive levels of thinking are emphasized, be sure the assessments clearly reflect those criteria)*	OBJECTIVES *Specific and measurable concepts to be learned—not the activities students perform to learn:* • *Specific skills, knowledge, and processes* • *Emphasized during instruction* • *Identified beforehand* • *Appropriate assessment techniques must be chosen for the assessment procedures* ACTIVITIES	• *Attends specifically to good pedagogy by focusing on students' prior knowledge, promoting high-level thinking, employing authentic assessment, and facilitating transfer through metacognition* • *Each element of the lesson perspective phrased in terms of what the student will do or learn* *(The information in the lesson perspective here is carried over to the Steps and Procedures of the Interdisciplinary Lesson Plan.)* ENGAGING THE LEARNER: EXPLORING PRIOR KNOWLEDGE: EXPLORING NEW IDEAS/CONCEPTS: ELABORATING ON NEW LEARNING: ASSESSING STUDENT UNDERSTANDING: CLOSURE/REFLECTION:
	LESSON 2	**LESSON 2 PERSPECTIVE**
RESOURCES AND MATERIALS: Any materials or tools that could be appropriately used for inquiry, but not limited to electronic and print reference materials, access to facilities such as tech or science labs, and human resources, such as persons to interview or to whom students can present.	OBJECTIVES ACTIVITIES	ENGAGING THE LEARNER: EXPLORING PRIOR KNOWLEDGE: EXPLORING NEW IDEAS/CONCEPTS: ELABORATING ON NEW LEARNING: ASSESSING STUDENT UNDERSTANDING: CLOSURE/REFLECTION:

(Continued)

TEMPLATE FOR UNIT PLANNING MAP (Continued)

	LESSON 3	LESSON 3 PERSPECTIVE
	OBJECTIVES ACTIVITIES	ENGAGING THE LEARNER: EXPLORING PRIOR KNOWLEDGE: EXPLORING NEW IDEAS/CONCEPTS: ELABORATING ON NEW LEARNING: ASSESSING STUDENT UNDERSTANDING: CLOSURE/REFLECTION:
	LESSON 4	LESSON 4 PERSPECTIVE
	OBJECTIVES ACTIVITIES	ENGAGING THE LEARNER: EXPLORING PRIOR KNOWLEDGE: EXPLORING NEW IDEAS/CONCEPTS: ELABORATING ON NEW LEARNING: ASSESSING STUDENT UNDERSTANDING: CLOSURE/REFLECTION:
	LESSON 5	LESSON 5 PERSPECTIVE
	OBJECTIVES ACTIVITIES	ENGAGING THE LEARNER: EXPLORING PRIOR KNOWLEDGE: EXPLORING NEW IDEAS/CONCEPTS: ELABORATING ON NEW LEARNING: ASSESSING STUDENT UNDERSTANDING: CLOSURE/REFLECTION:
	LESSON 6	LESSON 6 PERSPECTIVE
	OBJECTIVES ACTIVITIES	ENGAGING THE LEARNER: EXPLORING PRIOR KNOWLEDGE: EXPLORING NEW IDEAS/CONCEPTS: ELABORATING ON NEW LEARNING: ASSESSING STUDENT UNDERSTANDING: CLOSURE/REFLECTION:

TEMPLATE FOR UNIT OVERVIEW

UNIT AT A GLANCE

CURRICULUM AREA(S):

GRADE LEVEL(S):

Foundation of the unit (same as the Unit Planning Map)

UNIT GOALS AND OBJECTIVES

Students will . . .

Objectives phrased as "Students will . . ." and naturally evolve from the unit designer's understanding of the nature of the integrated content and the established standards associated with that content

RESOURCES AND MATERIALS

Any tool that could be appropriately used for inquiry, including but not limited to electronic and print reference material, access to facilities such as tech or science labs, and human resources such as persons to interview or to whom students can present

STANDARDS ADDRESSED

- *Standards reflected in the objectives*
- *Fuel for integration of instruction*

LANGUAGE ARTS	MATHEMATICS
SCIENCE	TECHNOLOGY
SOCIAL STUDIES	VISUAL ARTS
EVALUATION PLAN	EXTENSIONS
• *Keep feedback on learning objectives in mind throughout the unit* • *Establish what excellence looks like and use it as a basis for developing rubrics that will be used to assess student understanding of each objective.*	*Activities support transfer of knowledge and promote student metacognition.*

INTERDISCIPLINARY LESSONS

Week 1: Objectives: • *Phrased in terms of "At the end of the lesson, the student will be able to . . ."* • *Derived from the standards addressed* • *Measurable with some form of authentic assessment*	Week 1 Activities *Inquiry based and designed to meet the weekly unit objectives*
Week 2: Objectives: • *Phrased in terms of "At the end of the lesson, the student will be able to . . ."* • *Derived from the standards addressed* • *Measurable with some form of authentic assessment*	Week 2 Activities *Inquiry based and designed to meet the weekly unit objectives*

(Continued)

TEMPLATE FOR UNIT OVERVIEW (Continued)	
Week 3: Objectives: • *Phrased in terms of "At the end of the lesson, the student will be able to . . ."* • *Derived from the standards addressed* • *Measurable with some form of authentic assessment*	Week 3 Activities *Inquiry based and designed to meet the weekly unit objectives*
Week 4: Objectives: • *Phrased in terms of "At the end of the lesson, the student will be able to . . ."* • *Derived from the standards addressed* • *Measurable with some form of authentic assessment*	Week 4 Activities *Inquiry based and designed to meet the weekly unit objectives*

CREATING THE MOST EFFECTIVE INTEGRATED UNIT PLAN

Effectively integrating content areas requires that the nature of each be understood by the unit designer or designers. Once you begin to use the strategies and templates offered in this book to develop your own integrated units, you can evaluate each aspect of your design by employing the Teacher's Unit Plan Self-Evaluation Rubric shown on pages 12–14.

"Money, Money, Money" and "Earthquakes"

Following are two sample interdisciplinary units. Each unit may be used as is or adjusted to fit the particular needs of your classroom.

TEMPLATE FOR INTERDISCIPLINARY LESSON PLAN	

LESSON AT A GLANCE	
CURRICULUM AREA(S): GRADE LEVEL(S): LESSON DURATION: PREPARATION, RESOURCES, AND MATERIALS: *Refers to the information that needs to be identified before the lesson begins*	
INSTRUCTIONAL OBJECTIVES	**ONGOING ASSESSMENT**
• *Statement of the observable behaviors that the student will demonstrate by the end of the lesson (referring neither to the activity that helps accomplish the learning nor to the teacher's behavior)* • *Written to complete the following: "At the end of the lesson, the student will be able to . . ."*	*Addresses throughout the lesson those observable behaviors that indicate that the objectives are being met (Ongoing assessment is continual assessment that provides the feedback necessary to fine-tune the instruction.)*
STANDARDS ADDRESSED	
LANGUAGE ARTS	**MATHEMATICS**
List of content standards and process skills addressed by the lesson or activity	*List of content standards and process skills addressed by the lesson or activity*
SCIENCE	**TECHNOLOGY**
List of content standards and process skills addressed by the lesson or activity	*List of content standards and process skills addressed by the lesson or activity*
SOCIAL STUDIES	**VISUAL ARTS**
List of content standards and process skills addressed by the lesson or activity	*List of content standards and process skills addressed by the lesson or activity*
STEPS/PROCEDURES	
1. ENGAGING THE LEARNER	**2. EXPLORING PRIOR KNOWLEDGE**
• *First step in the process of instructional delivery* • *Activities that motivate students to delve deeply into content*	*Activities that explore what experiences and understandings the student brings to the content (the place where prior knowledge is connected to the new learning)*

(Continued)

TEMPLATE FOR INTERDISCIPLINARY LESSON PLAN (Continued)

3. EXPLORING NEW IDEAS	4. ELABORATING ON NEW LEARNING
New content explored through strategies that facilitate active student learning, including inquiry, direct instruction, discovery, and demonstration	• *Activities that prompt students to create a new product as a result of their synthesis of the content as it relates to their lives* • *Teacher-supported independent and group work that encourages accuracy and success (guided practice)*
5. ASSESSING STUDENT UNDERSTANDING	**6. CLOSURE AND REFLECTION**
Multiple and varied opportunities for students to exhibit skills and knowledge needed to achieve objectives *(Rubrics and checklists are designed to objectively and consistently evaluate student progress.)*	*Student display of achievement: the opportunity for demonstration of accomplished objectives* *(During closure, the work can be examined, reviewed, summarized, organized, and so on.)*
7. METHODS FOR DIFFERENTIATION OF INSTRUCTION	**8. LESSON FOLLOW-UP AND TEACHER REFLECTION**
• *Addresses students' various learning styles, strengths, and abilities* • *Provides the different instructional methodologies teachers will need when concepts are not well understood and need to be retaught*	• *Follow-up: homework, independent practice, extensions, and so on* • *Reflection: what occurred during the lesson, what might be learned from perceived lesson weakness, and what changes could be made to strengthen the instruction*

TEACHER'S UNIT PLAN SELF-EVALUATION RUBRIC

Criteria Evaluated	1 **Novice** Beginning **No, Not Yet**	2 **Basic** Developing **Yes, But**	3 **Proficient** Accomplished **Yes**	4 **Advanced** Exemplary **Yes Plus**
Unit Objectives	Objectives do not clearly describe the unit's purpose (why it is being taught).	Some of the objectives successfully describe the unit's purpose (why it is being taught) but do not place the work to come within a real-world context.	Objectives describe the unit's purpose (why it is being taught) and place the work to come within a real-world context.	Objectives target the unit's purpose (why it is being taught) and place the work to come within a highly innovative and student-oriented, real-world context.

	1	**2**	**3**	**4**
	Novice	**Basic**	**Proficient**	**Advanced**
Criteria Evaluated	Beginning **No, Not Yet**	Developing **Yes, But**	Accomplished **Yes**	Exemplary **Yes Plus**
Unit Planning Map or Unit Overview	Map or overview is disorganized, is difficult to follow, and shows a poor understanding of the disciplines.	Map or overview shows some organization, is legible, and shows some knowledge of the disciplines.	Map or overview is organized, neat, and easy to follow, and shows an underlying understanding of the nature of the various disciplines.	Map or overview is highly concise and well written (under 2 pages), with a unique presentation that is easy to follow and demonstrates superior insight into the nature of the various disciplines.
Individual Lesson Plans	Individual lesson plans do not follow the inquiry lesson model template.	There are 3 individual lesson plans, each following the inquiry lesson model template.	There are 4–5 individual lesson plans, each following the inquiry lesson model template.	There are more than 5 individual lesson plans, each closely following the inquiry lesson model template.
Hands-On Inquiry Activities	Activities or tasks are demonstrated to the class rather than experienced by the class.	Activities or tasks involve the class in some degree of active learning.	Activities or tasks involve the entire class in active, meaningful, and relevant learning.	Creative and unusual activities or tasks involve the entire class in active, meaningful, and relevant learning.
Unit Integration	Subject areas are not integrated well.	2 subject areas are successfully integrated.	3 different subject areas are successfully integrated.	More than 3 different subject areas are successfully integrated.
Culminating Task Organizer	Organizer is incomplete and does not fully describe all criteria.	Organizer is complete but does not fully describe all criteria.	Organizer is complete and fully describes all criteria.	Organizer is comprehensive, is well written, and fully describes all criteria.

(Continued)

	1 **Novice** Beginning **No, Not Yet**	2 **Basic** Developing **Yes, But**	3 **Proficient** Accomplished **Yes**	4 **Advanced** Exemplary **Yes Plus**
Criteria Evaluated				
Assessment Plan	• Plan contains 1 rubric, but that rubric is not consistently valid. • Plan does not promote student reflection.	• Plan contains 1 well-designed rubric that validly assesses the unit. • Plan contains only 1 opportunity for student reflection.	• Plan contains more than 1 comprehensive rubric that provides ongoing and valid assessment. • Plan contains several opportunities for student reflection.	• Plan contains several rubrics that assess the work throughout the unit with a high degree of validity. • Plan contains numerous and varied opportunities for student reflection.

Table title: **TEACHER'S UNIT PLAN SELF-EVALUATION RUBRIC (Continued)**

MONEY, MONEY, MONEY: CULMINATING TASK ORGANIZER

CURRICULUM AREA(S): Language Arts, Mathematics, Social Studies

GRADE LEVEL(S): 2

PROJECT DURATION: 3–4 weeks

RESOURCES/MATERIALS: Store supply list, plastic groceries, pretend money, cash register

TASK/PROJECT DESCRIPTION

Students will set up and run a mock grocery store. Each student will be responsible for researching the prices of two items that are on the store supply list. Each student will be given a set amount of money each week and will be able to earn more by working in the store. Students will be responsible for tracking money they have spent each week and what they bought. Students will have to use estimating skills to decide whether or not they have enough money to purchase what they want on a given day. They will also need to budget their money so that it lasts one week.

STANDARDS ADDRESSED

LANGUAGE ARTS	MATHEMATICS
4. Spoken, written, and visual language for effective communication 12. Spoken, written, and visual language to accomplish one's own purposes	1. Numbers and operations

SOCIAL STUDIES

7. Production, distribution, and consumption

MONEY, MONEY, MONEY: CULMINATING TASK ORGANIZER (Continued)

TASK/PROJECT OBJECTIVES

COMPREHENSION OF CONCEPTS	SKILL AND PROCESS DEVELOPMENT
At the end of this project, students will be able to . . . – Increase their financial awareness – Budget their money	At the end of this project, students will be able to . . . – Add and subtract using money – Use estimation skills – Work collaboratively – Communicate orally

PRODUCTS AND/OR PERFORMANCES

GROUP PRODUCTS	INDIVIDUAL PRODUCTS	EXTENSIONS
– Team will collaborate to set up and run the mock store.	– Students will keep a running tally of the items purchased and money spent – Students will write a paragraph at the conclusion of the mock store project, discussing what they have learned.	– With the help of a family member, students must track the food bought and money spent in one week and orally share their findings with the class.

CRITERIA FOR TASK/PROJECT EVALUATION

GROUP PRODUCTS	INDIVIDUAL PRODUCTS	EXTENSIONS
– Store organization – Pricing – Inventory – Managing money	– Performance task assessment of students' spending, budgeting, and estimating skills – Research and accuracy of pricing for two assigned store supplies – Written paragraph of what they learned	– Presentation and data collection skills used to track family food spending

MONEY, MONEY, MONEY: ASSESSMENT RUBRIC

Criteria Evaluated	1 Novice Beginning No, Not Yet	2 Basic Developing Yes, But	3 Proficient Accomplished Yes	4 Advanced Exemplary Yes Plus
Problem solving by making change	The student needs guidance to pay the correct number of dimes and to make correct change.	The student needs prompting to pay the correct number of dimes and has difficulty counting to make correct change.	The student pays the correct number of dimes and counts to make change with occasional errors.	The student pays the correct number of dimes and counts to make correct change in pennies.

MONEY, MONEY, MONEY: UNIT PLANNING MAP

UNIT AT A GLANCE	LESSON 1: What's It Worth?	LESSON 1 PERSPECTIVE
TOPIC: Money CURRICULUM AREA(S): Mathematics, Language Arts, Social Studies GRADE LEVEL(S): 2 PROJECT DURATION: 4 weeks UNIT OBJECTIVES: At the end of the unit, students will be able to . . . – Add and subtract – Estimate – Work collaboratively – Communicate orally TECHNOLOGY: Students can use calculators to help add lengthy orders. ASSESSMENT: – Student self-assessments – Rubrics	OBJECTIVES: At the end of the lesson, students will be able to . . . – Compare and contrast coins – Match coin and value ACTIVITIES: – Students will examine coins with magnifying glass. – Students will learn coin rap song. – Students will create a Venn diagram.	ENGAGING THE LEARNER: Introduce students to pennies, dimes, nickels, and quarters. EXPLORING PRIOR KNOWLEDGE: Brainstorm about coins with students. EXPLORING NEW IDEAS/CONCEPTS: Students will learn value and recognition of coins through rap song and create a Venn diagram. ELABORATING ON NEW LEARNING: Students will play the coin game. ASSESSING STUDENT UNDERSTANDING: Teacher monitoring, questions. CLOSURE/REFLECTION: Student self-assessment.
	LESSON 2: Poem Book	**LESSON 2 PERSPECTIVE**
	OBJECTIVES: At the end of the lesson, students will be able to . . . – Differentiate various coins – Add various coin values ACTIVITIES: – In groups, students will write descriptive poems. – Students will illustrate each poem with coin stamps. – Students will add coin values at the end of the book.	ENGAGING THE LEARNER: Read poem with students. EXPLORING PRIOR KNOWLEDGE: Review coin identification. EXPLORING NEW IDEAS/CONCEPTS: Poem writing. ELABORATING ON NEW LEARNING: Illustrating with stamps. ASSESSING STUDENT UNDERSTANDING: Teacher monitoring. CLOSURE/REFLECTION: Student self-assessment.

MONEY, MONEY, MONEY: UNIT PLANNING MAP

	LESSON 3: Making Change	**LESSON 3 PERSPECTIVE**
	OBJECTIVES: At the end of the lesson, students will be able to . . . – Solve problems by making change ACTIVITIES: – Cooperative groups will label items with appropriate prices. – Students will take turns buying and selling items.	ENGAGING THE LEARNER: Read *Market!* by Ted Lewin. Class discussion. EXPLORING PRIOR KNOWLEDGE: Review coin combinations to $1.00. EXPLORING NEW IDEAS/ CONCEPTS: Explain the multiple meanings of the word *change*. ELABORATING ON NEW LEARNING: Cooperative groups will label items with prices. Students will buy, sell, and make change. ASSESSING STUDENT UNDERSTANDING: Teacher monitoring, Assessment Rubric. CLOSURE/REFLECTION: Questioning and journal activity.
	LESSON 4: Money in the Bank	**LESSON 4 PERSPECTIVE**
	OBJECTIVES: At the end of the lesson, students will be able to . . . – Use addition and subtraction ACTIVITIES: – Students will create their own bank used for game. – Students will create play money in the bank.	ENGAGING THE LEARNER: Review and discuss coins. EXPLORING PRIOR KNOWLEDGE: The class discusses prior knowledge of coins. EXPLORING NEW IDEAS/ CONCEPTS: Demonstrate adding and subtracting with coins. ELABORATING ON NEW LEARNING: Students will play game. ASSESSING STUDENT UNDERSTANDING: Student written work, addition and subtraction problems, questioning. CLOSURE/REFLECTION: Use coins in game and add to math center.

EARTHQUAKES: CULMINATING TASK ORGANIZER

CURRICULUM AREA(S): Language Arts, Mathematics, Technology, Visual Arts, Science, Social Studies

CUMULATING TASK/PROJECT TITLE: Earthquakes

GRADE LEVEL(S): 6

PROJECT DURATION: 4 weeks

RESOURCES/MATERIALS: Computers with Internet access, textbooks, videos, journals, newspaper articles

TASK/PROJECT DESCRIPTION

Student groups of 4 or 5 will each represent a historical earthquake in the setting where it took place (that is, country, city, water, and so on). Each group will research the origin of its occurrence and make a map noting the areas of the setting that the earthquake affected. (Was it positive or negative?) Groups will also keep a daily journal of the entire process and will continue to document the reactions of the people living in the area. At the end of the unit, each group will present its research by making a mural of the final results about the area affected. Individually, students will also write a research paper that includes their results.

STANDARDS ADDRESSED

LANGUAGE ARTS	VISUAL ARTS
1. Reading to build understanding 4. Spoken, written, and visual language for effective communication 12. Spoken, written, and visual language to accomplish one's own purposes	1. Understanding and applying media, techniques, and processes 4. Understanding the visual arts in relation to history and cultures
MATHEMATICS	**SCIENCE**
1. Numbers and operations 4. Measurement 5. Data analysis and probability	A. Science as inquiry C. Life science D. Earth and space
TECHNOLOGY	**SOCIAL STUDIES**
1. Basic operations and concepts 3. Technology productivity tools 4. Technology communications tools	2. Time, continuity, and change 3. People, places, and environments

TASK/PROJECT OBJECTIVES

COMPREHENSION OF CONCEPTS	SKILL AND PROCESS DEVELOPMENT
At the end of this project, students will be able to . . . • Describe the process by which earthquakes develop and are defined • Demonstrate comprehension of how earthquakes affect different areas and society • Demonstrate effects of the earthquake. • Reproduce research results using artistic media	At the end of this project, students will be able to . . . • Create maps • Create/evaluate graphs • Research a topic • Display positive team skills and cooperation

EARTHQUAKES: CULMINATING TASK ORGANIZER

PRODUCTS AND/OR PERFORMANCES

GROUP PRODUCTS	INDIVIDUAL PRODUCTS	EXTENSIONS
• Maps of area the earthquake hit and surrounding areas affected • Mural of results • Oral presentation	• Research paper • Research notebooks and notes • Daily journals	• Organize a tag sale and donate proceeds to recent earthquake/tsunami victims

CRITERIA FOR TASK/PROJECT EVALUATION

GROUP PRODUCTS	INDIVIDUAL PRODUCTS	EXTENSIONS
Map of Affected Area • Accuracy • Neatness • Content • Readability/User Friendliness • Color • Originality **Mural** • Accuracy • Group Cooperation • Content • Color • Originality **Oral Presentation** • Eye contact • Group cooperation • Content • Articulation • Visual aids • Organization	**Research Paper** • Quality of content • Organization of data • Conclusions • Neatness • Spelling and grammar • Inclusion of parts **Research Notebook** • Organization • Neatness **Daily Journals** • Content • Neatness	**Organization of Tag Sale** • Grouping of items • Pricing of items • Methods of collecting money • Methods of recording sales

EARTHQUAKES: UNIT PLANNING MAP

UNIT AT A GLANCE	LESSON 1: What Is an Earthquake?	LESSON 1 PERSPECTIVE
TOPIC: Earthquakes CURRICULUM AREA(S): Science, Language Arts, Mathematics, Social Studies, Technology, and Visual Arts GRADE LEVEL(S): 6 PROJECT DURATION: 4 weeks UNIT OBJECTIVES: At the end of the unit, students will be able to . . . – Describe how earthquakes are defined and developed – List ways in which earthquakes affect different areas and society – Determine how earthquakes are measured and recorded – Determine where different places are on a map – Identify distances between places on a map – Demonstrate correct use of a key/legend – Orient a map using a compass – Reproduce research results – Compare, analyze, and assess data – Conduct purposeful research via the Internet – Gather knowledge of a given task TECHNOLOGY: – Internet for research ASSESSMENT: – Rubrics – Teacher observation	OBJECTIVES: At the end of the lesson, students will be able to . . . – Describe how earthquakes are developed and are defined – Depict locations of earthquakes ACTIVITIES: Students will . . . – Complete worksheets	ENGAGING THE LEARNER: Show a movie clip to students. EXPLORING PRIOR KNOWLEDGE: Ask if anyone knows what an earthquake is or how it is formed. EXPLORING NEW IDEAS/CONCEPTS: Students will research earthquakes in textbooks and/or Web sites provided. ELABORATING ON NEW LEARNING: In groups, students will research data on earthquakes. ASSESSING STUDENT UNDERSTANDING: Worksheet about earthquakes. CLOSURE/REFLECTION: Completion of worksheet.
	LESSON 2: Effects of an Earthquake	**LESSON 2 PERSPECTIVE**
	OBJECTIVES: At the end of the lesson, students will be able to . . . – List ways in which earthquakes affect different areas and society ACTIVITIES: Students will . . . – Visit "trigger an earthquake" on the interactive Web site http://www.nationalgeographic.com – Complete the earthquake crossword puzzle after researching http://earthquakes.usgs.gov	ENGAGING THE LEARNER: Show various photographs of places that were affected by an earthquake. EXPLORING PRIOR KNOWLEDGE: Ask students if they know how earthquakes affect different surroundings and settings. Ask students if they know of a famous earthquake and its impact on society. EXPLORING NEW IDEAS/CONCEPTS: Students will read a variety of accounts of famous earthquake disasters. Students will then go to 2 Web sites (nationalgeographic.com and earthquakes.usgs.gov) and learn more about earthquakes and the hazards of living in certain areas. ASSESSING STUDENT UNDERSTANDING: Completion of the earthquake crossword puzzle. CLOSURE/REFLECTION: Discussion of Web sites, pictures, and crossword puzzle.

EARTHQUAKES: UNIT PLANNING MAP

LESSON 3: Reading and Making Maps	LESSON 3 PERSPECTIVE
OBJECTIVES: At the end of this lesson, students will be able to . . . – Determine where different places are on a map – Identify distances between places on a map – Demonstrate correct use of a key/legend ACTIVITIES: Students will . . . – Draw a map of Connecticut that includes a key and legend – Plot earthquakes that have occurred in Connecticut on the map	ENGAGING THE LEARNER: Show a few examples of maps, discussing important features of a map, such as key, legend, and scale. EXPLORING PRIOR KNOWLEDGE: Ask what students know about maps, including keys, legends, and scale. EXPLORING NEW IDEAS/CONCEPTS: Hand out a variety of different kinds of maps. What are the differences and similarities between them? ELABORATING ON NEW LEARNING: Discuss and chart differences and similarities between the different kinds of maps. ASSESSING STUDENT UNDERSTANDING: Completion of chart as a class; completion, accuracy, and presentation of group maps. CLOSURE/REFLECTION: Presentation of group maps.
LESSON 4: How to Research Information	**LESSON 4 PERSPECTIVE**
OBJECTIVES: At the end of this lesson, students will be able to . . . – Compare, analyze, and assess data – Conduct purposeful research via the Internet ACTIVITIES: Students will . . . – Research via the Internet – Retrieve images via the Internet – Copy, cut, and paste relevant information and images	ENGAGING THE LEARNER: Explain to students that they will be conducting a scavenger hunt utilizing the Internet to do research. EXPLORING PRIOR KNOWLEDGE: Ask students if they have ever used the Internet for research. If so, how? EXPLORING NEW IDEAS/CONCEPTS: Give students a list of tasks to research on the Internet. Students will then collect data for assigned tasks. ELABORATING ON NEW LEARNING: Show students how to copy, cut, and paste images and information. Also show students how to retrieve new facts and ideas from the Internet. ASSESSING STUDENT UNDERSTANDING: Teacher observation, amount of content/information collected. CLOSURE/REFLECTION: Sharing of collected data/information.

(Continued)

EARTHQUAKES: UNIT PLANNING MAP (Continued)

	LESSON 5: Writing a Research Paper	**LESSON 5 PERSPECTIVE**
	OBJECTIVES: At the end of this lesson, students will be able to . . . – Reproduce research results ACTIVITIES: Students will . . . – Research a topic – Write a research paper together	ENGAGING THE LEARNER: Show a few pictures of the deadliest earthquakes in history. EXPLORING PRIOR KNOWLEDGE: Ask students if they know what the deadliest earthquake was, where it occurred, and how many fatalities there were. EXPLORING NEW IDEAS/CONCEPTS: Give students a list of Web sites, textbooks, and other resources to use. In groups, students will research and collect data on their given aspect of the earthquake. After researching, the class will come together and share data. Then students will write the research paper together using proper guidelines. ASSESSING STUDENT UNDERSTANDING: Teacher observation, amount and relevance of information collected. CLOSURE/REFLECTION: Finished product of research paper.
	LESSON 6: Mural Making	**LESSON 6 PERSPECTIVE**
	OBJECTIVES: At the end of this lesson, students will be able to . . . – Demonstrate effects of an earthquake using artistic media ACTIVITIES: Students will . . . – Create a mural that demonstrates the effects of the earthquake on a particular setting	ENGAGING THE LEARNER: Show some examples of murals. EXPLORING PRIOR KNOWLEDGE: Ask students if they know the particular name of the pictures. EXPLORING NEW IDEAS/CONCEPTS: Explain the components and procedures of making a mural. ELABORATING ON NEW LEARNING: Students will make an authentic mural based on the effects of their earthquake. Encourage students to be creative. ASSESSING STUDENT UNDERSTANDING: Teacher observation during mural-making process, completion and accuracy of mural, creative use of media. CLOSURE/REFLECTION: Presentation of mural depicting earthquake's effects.

Organizing Instruction for Meaning

Planning for Learning and Achievement

MAKING LEARNING MEANINGFUL

Merely being able to carry out mathematical computation or to recall a list of word definitions represents a kind of learning often referred to as "surface knowledge." Such surface knowledge cannot be equated with the deeper learning known as "concept comprehension." Tasks and activities designed for surface knowledge alone do not develop a student's critical thinking skills (intellectual engagement) and therefore cannot be considered meaningful activities.

Truly meaningful learning occurs when an individual applies the surface knowledge and basic skills learned to realistic, contextual problems. It is through the act of searching for solutions that true comprehension takes place. Whether or not a concept has been truly learned can best be evaluated through concept application and demonstration of the learner's ability to solve those challenging problems in new and unfamiliar situations.

WORKING WITH HOW THE BRAIN WORKS

The past several decades have witnessed an explosion of knowledge in the field of the neurosciences. We humans have always been fascinated and mystified by the ways in which the brain functions, but we were not able to "see" a living, functioning human brain at work until the 1980s. Vividly colored pictures from imaging techniques such as positron emission tomography (PET) and functional magnetic resonance imaging (fMRI) give us concrete images of what previously we could only imagine. This technology now affords neuroscientists the opportunity to monitor brain activity in healthy, living human subjects by employing radioactively labeled oxygen and glucose to measure rates of brain energy metabolism.

Research by scientists such as Marty Sereno (1991a, 1991b, 1999, 2005) and Stanislas Dehaene (1997, 2001), whose work deals with the neurobiology of language and mathematics, appears to indicate that many of our traditional instructional methodologies work in opposition to the brain's natural way of processing new knowledge.

Howard Gardner (1983), Robert Sternberg (1996), Sternberg, Forsythe, Hedlund, Horvath, Snook, Williams, et al. (2000), Renate and Geoffrey Caine (1997a), Caine, Caine, and McClintic (2002), Pat Wolfe (2001), Daniel Goleman (1995), and Eric Jensen (1998, 2005) are only a few of the educators who have examined new discoveries in neuroscience for their possible implications for learning. (See Figure 2.1.)

Isolating subject areas from their naturally integrated context and presenting them to learners as independent and discrete units run counter to the brain's intrinsically integrative processing of information. Psychologists and cognitive researchers such as Gardner (1999, 2005), Sternberg (1996), and Sternberg et al. (2000) have conducted studies supporting the idea that implementation of practical, creative, or interpersonal aspects of intelligence will enhance meaningful learning. Other research evidence appears to indicate that the brain innately seeks patterns to form connections (Caine & Caine, 1997a).

What this means in educational terms is that instead of emphasizing the memorization of isolated skills and facts, educators will have greater success concentrating on the integration of the concepts that underlie the new learning. Research appears to support an integrated instructional methodology that is student centered rather than teacher centered, and problem based rather than solution based (Ronis, 2007c). With such innovative methodology, the student becomes the active participant in the process, while the teacher's role evolves into that of facilitator or guide.

Emotions

Emotions, critical components in the learning equation, have long been excluded from the curriculum. Since emotion drives attention, and attention is

Figure 2.1   Designing Instruction for the Brain's Way of Learning

- Use a multiplicity of assorted learning approaches.
- Employ active rather than passive participation in new knowledge construction.
- Schedule extra time for processing information through metacognitive activities such as reflection.
- Facilitate emotional, intellectual, and physical connections to the content.
- Allow for socialization in an environment that supports risk taking.

what drives learning (Sylwester, 1995), neglecting the role of emotion hampers the learning process.

Social Interaction

Another learning component often ignored in traditional instruction is that of socialization. Traditional instructional methods that isolate students and create competitive situations are counterproductive for processing new knowledge. By encouraging a learning environment of positive interdependence in which the achievement of a common goal is mutually beneficial, teachers help students to process new information in their own way and at their own pace.

Learning that is brain compatible is learning that takes advantage of the innate search for meaning and relevancy. Instructors can turn that search into an effective teaching methodology that educates through the presentation of problem situations in need of solutions. Such problem situations do not have a single correct answer but rather ask students to learn through the act of trying to resolve those problems. Figure 2.2 summarizes the findings of cognitive researchers and neuroscientists as they relate to classroom practice.

COMPREHENSIVE DESIGN

When developing interdisciplinary inquiry units, always keep the final outcome in mind: what students should know and be able to do as well as what behaviors, skills, habits, and so on they must exhibit at the unit's end to demonstrate their new learning and understanding. Think about the final assessment and then work backward from that assessment. (It is important for students to know from the very beginning what they are expected to bring to the unit task and what they will need to know at its close.) For this reason, it is best to begin a unit plan with the design of its Culminating Task.

The Culminating Task is the spark that ignites the students' interest. It is the vehicle that drives the learning and around which the new learning revolves. To be meaningful and real world, the task must have the kind of relevancy that piques learner curiosity. It is the motivation that engages students in a quest for answers. Once the activity or project has been created, the content standards and/or results that are being addressed through that task must be identified. The assessment, evidence of learning, and specific lessons are planned out afterward and usually follow the logic of "what skills and knowledge will students need in order to complete this task successfully?" Figure 2.3 lists the central questions that drive the design of the Culminating Task.

PERFORMANCE TASKS AND PRODUCTS

By identifying the kinds of performance tasks or products students will complete to demonstrate their learning, the Culminating Task helps to focus both student interest and teacher objectives. Figure 2.4 provides a list of prompts that can help individual teachers or a group of cooperating teachers design meaningful Culminating Tasks.

Figure 2.2   Planning for Meaning Making

Research Suggests . . .	Corresponding Teaching Strategies
Brain Growth and Development	
Windows of opportunity represent critical periods during which the brain demands certain types of input to create or consolidate neural networks. This input then results in the physical alteration of the brain's structure.	By understanding the different windows of opportunity for growth, teachers can plan how best to approach the content and skills in their curriculum so as to provide a supportive, enriched, and brain-friendly classroom environment.
Learning engages the entire mind/body physiology. Physical development, personal comfort, and emotional state affect one's ability to learn. The search for meaning and connections is innate.	Children mature at different rates; chronological age may not reflect a student's development or readiness to learn. Therefore, the pedagogy must allow for instructional differentiation.
Memory and Recall	
Past experiences influence new learning. What we already know acts as a filter, helping us attend to those things that have meaning and relevancy, and discard those that do not.	Integrating curriculum while also connecting it to students' prior experiences helps those learners make relevant connections among the content areas, thereby improving learning retention.
	Information for lessons and activities must be contextual so as to encourage meaningful connections.
	Relevant, task-centered discussion is critical to the memory process, since that discussion helps to maintain student focus while enhancing meaning and relevancy.
Emotions and Learning	
Emotions and cognition cannot be separated within the mind/body. How students feel about a learning situation determines the amount of attention they devote to it. Emotion drives attention, which in turn drives the learning process.	Promote emotional security by establishing a positive climate that encourages students to take appropriate risks while learning (as with small group work).
	Encourage students to be aware of their feelings and how their emotions affect their learning.
Multisensory Involvement	
The brain makes new neural connections when it is actively involved in situations that are both interesting and challenging.	Classrooms should be busy, interactive environments. Consistently use a multisensory approach to keep students actively engaged in their learning.

Figure 2.3   Central Questions for the Design of the Culminating Task

- How can I promote challenge and intrigue for my students while keeping the level of complexity within their reach?
- What specific knowledge and skills will enable the unit learning? (What are the various unit goals, objectives, and content standards?)
- What appropriate activities and experiences need to be designed?
- What teaching or coaching skills are needed?
- What constitutes sound evidence of achievement?
- What must be observable to judge that learning has occurred?

Figure 2.4   Brainstorming Prompts for Authentic and Meaningful Performance Tasks and Performances

- ✓ How do students use the skills and knowledge that scientists, engineers, designers, and others use in the performance of this task or creation of this product?
- ✓ How does this task or product relate to the developmental needs and interests of the students?
- ✓ What are the specific qualities and characteristics that must be included in the evidence of learning?
- ✓ What specific ways of documenting production, perception, and reflection will be used?

CULMINATING TASK ORGANIZER

Good evidence of understanding requires thoughtful planning. The Culminating Task Organizer helps to ensure that all significant aspects of unit design have been included in the unit plan. If certain components of the Culminating Task Organizer are blank, missing, or not in alignment after the final activity has been crafted, it becomes clear exactly where further unit refinement is needed. (A blank Culminating Task Organizer template is included in Appendix II: Planning Forms.)

Organizing Instruction for Meaning: Planning for Learning and Achievement

To achieve thorough comprehension of unit content, the design of inquiry tasks must be headed in a direction that requires understanding for practical life issues. Following are questions that all good inquiry task designers must address:

- Why are we doing this?
- Where is it headed?
- Why does it matter?

Just because a task, a unit, or an assessment is performance based, it does not automatically follow that students will truly understand the concept. Figure 2.5 lists questions that teachers can ask to judge whether or not a task provides opportunity for students to evidence understanding and skills acquisition.

VALUING CONTENT AND STUDENT PERSPECTIVE

Effective instructional planning begins by building instruction around student interest within a relevant context. A meaningful task has students draw on experience and knowledge derived from multiple content areas the same way people are called on to bring their knowledge and experience to bear when problem solving and planning in their daily lives. This helps build student understanding and is also just about the only feasible way to address the myriad standards established by professional and content organizations as well as individual states. (See Appendix I: Content Area Standards.)

Figure 2.5   Measuring the Validity of a Culminating Task

After drafting a task, ask yourself the following questions:

- ✓ Could students successfully complete the proposed work but still not achieve understanding?
- ✓ Could evidence of comprehension still be at issue or in question for different reasons regardless of how well or how poorly the proposed work is done?
- ✓ What exactly would I consider evidence of understanding to look like?
- ✓ Where should I look and what should I look for in judging whether or not understanding is present or emerging?
- ✓ What must students eventually show me to prove that they now know, understand, and can do well?
- ✓ What represents sound evidence of understanding (versus mere familiarity and/or recall)?
- ✓ How will I distinguish understanding from misunderstanding, insight from rehashed teacher and textbook statements, and thoughtful from haphazard control of what was taught?

Next, decide on the manner in which the evidence of learning will be assessed by asking the following questions:

- ✓ What kind of authentic and alternative assessment measures will be used?
- ✓ What criteria (rubric and benchmarks) will be used for assessing students' products?
- ✓ Will the products be the kind that fit the portfolio profile? (Do they conform to the requirements and/or parameters of a portfolio?)

CHAPTER TWO | Sample Units

"Theme Park" and "Write Your Own Textbook"

Following are two sample interdisciplinary units. Each unit may be used as is or adjusted to fit the particular needs of your classroom.

THEME PARK: CULMINATING TASK ORGANIZER

LESSON AT A GLANCE

CURRICULUM AREA(S): Language Arts, Mathematics, Technology, Science, Social Studies, Visual Arts

GRADE LEVEL(S): 6–8

PROJECT DURATION: 5 weeks

RESOURCES/MATERIALS: Internet access, supplies for experiments and artwork, books, videos, journals, paper, PowerPoint

TASK/PROJECT DESCRIPTION

Student teams have been chosen to develop a new theme park! Utilizing knowledge and experience with the laws of physics and motion, each team will develop a proposal for a new and exciting theme park. The team will be given a region in which to create the park, and each team member will research one state from that region. Based on the culture, history, folklore, clothing, food, or music of that region, students will come up with an appropriate theme for the park. Every student will keep a journal for reflections and lab notes. In addition, each team will be responsible for the following:
  - Build a successful prototype and a diagram of one ride that demonstrates knowledge of physics topics to share with the committee. The team will describe in a few paragraphs how its model reflects the three laws of motion.
  - Design an original and creative park map that reflects the theme of the park and includes ten points of interest.
  - Create a PowerPoint presentation detailing all safety measures and features of the theme park.

STANDARDS ADDRESSED

LANGUAGE ARTS	TECHNOLOGY
1. Reading to build understanding 4. Spoken, written, and visual language for effective communication 6. Application of language structure and conventions to create, critique, and discuss 8. Technological and information resources to gather and synthesize information and to create and communicate knowledge	3. Technology productivity tools 4. Technology communications tools 5. Technology research tools
MATHEMATICS	**SCIENCE**
2. Algebra 4. Measurement 5. Data analysis and probability 6. Problem solving 10. Representation	A. Science as inquiry B. Physical science E. Science and technology

(Continued)

THEME PARK: CULMINATING TASK ORGANIZER (Continued)

SOCIAL STUDIES	VISUAL ARTS
1. Culture 3. People, places, and environments	1. Understanding and applying media, techniques, and processes 6. Making connections between visual arts and other disciplines

TASK/PROJECT OBJECTIVES

COMPREHENSION OF CONCEPTS	SKILL AND PROCESS DEVELOPMENT
At the end of this project, students will be to able to demonstrate comprehension of . . . – Newton's three laws of motion – Inertia, force, acceleration, action and reaction – Roller coaster physics – Ride safety – Folklore and culture of a specific region of the United States – Map making – Microsoft PowerPoint	At the end of this project, students will be able to demonstrate . . . – Written and oral communication – Technological awareness and comprehension – Research and organisation of data – Team approach to problem solving – Positive interdependence – Individual accountability – Critical thinking

PRODUCTS AND/OR PERFORMANCES

GROUP PRODUCTS	INDIVIDUAL PRODUCTS	EXTENSIONS
– Model of ride – Diagram of proposed ride – Theme park map – PowerPoint presentation of safety issues	– Journal – Research on assigned state – Participation in discussions and activities	– Guest speaker from amusement park to talk about safety – Engineer of rides to sit on committee and speak to class – Field trip tour of an amusement park – Advertisement or marketing strategy for park – A second prototype of a proposed ride

CRITERIA FOR TASK/PROJECT EVALUATION

GROUP PRODUCTS	INDIVIDUAL PRODUCTS	EXTENSIONS
– Working prototype of ride follows rules of physics. – Diagram is detailed and reflects knowledge of physics. – Park map is organized, neat, detailed, and free of errors. – PowerPoint presentation includes information about safety issues.	– Journal is organized and insightful and includes all necessary lab notes and reflections. – Research on assigned state is thorough and properly documented. – There is evidence of participation in class discussion and activities.	– Teams may be awarded extra points for working on extension activities.

THEME PARK: DESIGN RUBRIC				
Criteria Evaluated	**1** **Novice** Beginning **No, Not Yet**	**2** **Basic** Developing **Yes, But**	**3** **Proficient** Accomplished **Yes**	**4** **Advanced** Exemplary **Yes Plus**
Organization	Project is not organized, and proper format was not followed.	Project is organized, but proper format was not followed.	Project demonstrates satisfactory organization, and proper format is followed.	Project demonstrates sophisticated organization, follows proper format, and is unique and engaging.
Design of ride (Diagram and prototype)	Diagram is not labeled and legible, and prototype is not a working model of a park ride.	Diagram is labeled and legible, but prototype is not a working representation.	Diagram is legible and labeled. Prototype displays one or more aspects of the physics topics.	Diagram is complex and precise, and model is a smoothly working prototype that displays rigorous knowledge of physics topics.
Park map	Park map does not colorfully or accurately represent the region. It includes less than 6 points of interest and has no map key.	Park map is somewhat colorful, accurate, and detailed, but it includes no more than 7 points of interest and may lack a map key.	Park map clearly and accurately represents the region. It includes 8–10 points of interest and a map key.	Park map is complex yet precise, colorful, detailed, and clearly represents the region, with more than 10 points of interest and a map key.
PowerPoint presentation	Presentation does not include 5 slides and does not outline safety measures of the park.	Presentation includes 5 slides, but little attempt was made to include safety features of park.	Presentation includes 5 slides outlining the safety features of the park.	Elegant presentation includes more than 5 slides and perceptively addresses all safety issues of the park.
Creativity	Theme park is not presented in a unique or engaging manner.	Theme park presentation is satisfactory, but little attempt was made to be creative.	Theme park is creative, and presentation was satisfactory.	Complex theme park is designed and presented in a powerfully creative and unique manner.

THEME PARK: MAP RUBRIC				
Criteria Evaluated	**1** **Novice** Beginning **No, Not Yet**	**2** **Basic** Developing **Yes, But**	**3** **Proficient** Accomplished **Yes**	**4** **Advanced** Exemplary **Yes Plus**
Organization	Park map is not legible or easy to follow, and numerous errors are apparent.	Park map can be followed, but little effort was made to write legibly.	Park map is legible and easy to follow.	Park map is innovative, explicit, and very easy to follow.
Theme	Park theme does not reflect the region, and an insufficient amount of research is evident.	Park theme represents the region, but more research is needed.	Park theme satisfactorily represents the region and is supported by adequate research.	Park theme elegantly represents the region, as supported by extensive research of that area of the United States.
Points of interest	Park map includes fewer than 5 points of interest.	Park map includes 6–9 points of interest, but descriptions and pictures are missing.	Park map includes all 10 points of interest with descriptions and illustrations.	Park map includes more than 10 points of interest, each with a detailed description and represented by a masterful drawing or exemplary picture.
Map key	Park map is not proportional, and map key is missing.	Park map is for the most part proportional to the actual size of the park, but no attempt was made to design a map key.	Park map is in proportion and includes a map key.	Park map is expertly drawn in proportion to the actual size of the amusement park and contains a map key with accurate measurements.
Creativity	Park map is not designed in a creative or unique manner and needs considerable work.	Park map shows some creativity, but could have displayed more effort.	Park map shows some creativity.	Park map is masterfully designed using creative, colorful, and unique design elements.

THEME PARK: JOURNAL RUBRIC

Criteria Evaluated	1 Novice Beginning No, Not Yet	2 Basic Developing Yes, But	3 Proficient Accomplished Yes	4 Advanced Exemplary Yes Plus
Is the student's journal well organized, clear, and legible?	Journal is not well organized, clear, or legible.	Journal is well organized, but little attempt was made to be clear or legible.	Journal is organized and legible.	Journal is sophisticated, concisely organized, highly legible, and easy to follow.
Did the student include all lab notes from experiments and class discussion?	Lab notes are incomplete and unclear.	Lab notes are complete, but some parts are imprecise.	All lab notes are complete.	Extensive lab notes are highly detailed, clear, and complete.
Did the student include reflections from activities and discussions throughout the unit?	Reflections are incomplete and do not show evidence of higher order thinking.	Reflections are included, but there is little evidence of higher order thinking.	Reflections are complete and thoughtful.	Intuitive reflections are included in the journal, and all entries demonstrate sophisticated thinking.
Did the student include research about his or her assigned state with proper documentation?	Research is not included in the journal, and there is no documentation.	Research is included, but there is little or no documentation.	Research with documentation is included.	Research is exemplary and thorough and includes proper documentation.
Is there a group and individual self-assessment in the journal?	Student did not complete the self-assessment.	Student's self-assessment was honest, but assessment was incomplete.	Student's self-assessment was honest, accurate, and complete.	Student's penetrating self-assessment honestly and completely evaluates individual and group performance.

THEME PARK: UNIT PLANNING MAP

UNIT AT A GLANCE	LESSON 1: Amusement Parks: Past and Present	LESSON 1 PERSPECTIVE
TOPIC: Theme Parks CURRICULUM AREA(S): Science, Mathematics, Language Arts, Social Studies, Technology, Visual Arts GRADE LEVEL(S): 6–8 PROJECT DURATION: 5 weeks UNIT OBJECTIVES: At the end of the unit, students will be able to. . . – Understand the role of physics in everyday life and apply this knowledge to create a new theme park – Investigate theme parks of the past and gain an understanding of the culture of America at that time compared to today – Apply scientific and historical information to a real-world problem and present a proposal in an engaging and interesting manner; Web sites and CD-ROMs will be available for student learning	OBJECTIVES: Students will be able to . . . – Use information about theme parks of the past and present to generate questions that the unit study will answer. ACTIVITIES: – Students will conduct a research study of amusement parks and park rides using the Internet, books, videos, and computer games. They will look at the culture of America during the time of old parks like Coney Island through video, pictures, and books.	ENGAGING THE LEARNER: Students will see videos about amusement parks and look at park maps. EXPLORING PRIOR KNOWLEDGE: Students will complete a KWL chart. (What do you know, and what have you learned about amusement parks?) EXPLORING NEW IDEAS/CONCEPTS: Are there differences between old and new parks? ELABORATING ON NEW LEARNING: Students will come up with questions to be addressed during the unit about how park rides work. ASSESSING STUDENT UNDERSTANDING: Journals will be evaluated for notes, research, and questions. CLOSURE/REFLECTION: The culminating activity will be introduced, and teams will be assigned.
	LESSON 2: Inertia: Newton's First Law of Motion	**LESSON 2 PERSPECTIVE**
	OBJECTIVES: Students will be able to . . . – Complete various scientific experiments and draw conclusions from the results ACTIVITIES: – Students will take part in a series of experiments that involve inertia and Newton's first law.	ENGAGING THE LEARNER: Demonstrate inertia to students. EXPLORING PRIOR KNOWLEDGE: Who was Sir Isaac Newton? What do you know about motion? EXPLORING NEW IDEAS/CONCEPTS: What is the connection between inertia and theme parks? ELABORATING ON NEW LEARNING: Students will conduct experiments and draw conclusions. ASSESSING STUDENT UNDERSTANDING: Lab reports and class discussion will be assessed for understanding. CLOSURE/REFLECTION: Class discussion about inertia and lab results.

THEME PARK: UNIT PLANNING MAP		
UNIT AT A GLANCE	**LESSON 3: Force, Mass, and Acceleration: Newton's Second Law of Motion**	**LESSON 3 PERSPECTIVE**
TECHNOLOGY: – Students will use the Internet to investigate and research various topics. – Special Windows-based programs will be available for theme park simulations, and PowerPoint will be used for presentations. ASSESSMENT: Using rubrics, teacher will assess projects, presentations, journals, and cooperative group work.	OBJECTIVES: Students will be able to . . . – Discuss, explain, and demonstrate Newton's second law of motion ACTIVITIES: – Students will make observations from a science experiment using various materials and relate findings to the motion of park rides.	ENGAGING THE LEARNER: Ask "What makes something go?" Any misconceptions voiced during the discussion should be addressed during the teacher demonstration of Newton's second law of motion. EXPLORING PRIOR KNOWLEDGE: Students will recall what they did in the last lesson. EXPLORING NEW IDEAS/CONCEPTS: Demonstrate Newton's second law of motion. ELABORATING ON NEW LEARNING: What can you conclude about force, mass, and acceleration? Students will explore the second law through science labs. ASSESSING STUDENT UNDERSTANDING: Participation in labs or discussion in journals. CLOSURE/REFLECTION: Ask "What have you learned, and how can you apply this information to your theme park ride?"
	LESSON 4: Action and Reaction: Newton's Third Law of Motion	**LESSON 4 PERSPECTIVE**
	OBJECTIVES: Students will be able to . . . – Demonstrate Newton's third law of motion and be able to apply it to theme park physics ACTIVITIES: – Students will participate in a balloon rocket lab that demonstrates action and reaction. Teams will come up with an original lab activity that would help others understand the concept.	ENGAGING THE LEARNER: Balloon demonstration. EXPLORING PRIOR KNOWLEDGE: Ask "What do you know about balloons and air?" EXPLORING NEW IDEAS/CONCEPTS: Teams will conduct a lab experiment. ELABORATING ON NEW LEARNING: Create a new lab that shows the concept of action and reaction. ASSESSING STUDENT UNDERSTANDING: Labs, journals, class discussion. CLOSURE/REFLECTION: Work will begin on the park ride design.

WRITE YOUR OWN TEXTBOOK: CULMINATING TASK ORGANIZER

CURRICULUM AREA(S): Language Arts, Mathematics, Technology
GRADE LEVEL(S): 7 (accelerated)
PROJECT DURATION: 7 days
RESOURCES/MATERIALS: Textbook, computers with Microsoft Excel®, worksheets

TASK/PROJECT DESCRIPTION

After an introductory unit exploring fractions, pattern recognition, basic probability, and estimation of large numbers, students will create a textbook lesson explaining the rules of fractions. The lessons will demonstrate students' knowledge of the mechanics of fraction arithmetic (adding, subtracting, multiplying, and dividing), and each rule will be accompanied by an analytical explanation of *why* the rule works. Explanations can include diagrams and sample problems. Students will also construct problem sets containing problems appropriate to the content their lessons taught.

STANDARDS ADDRESSED

LANGUAGE ARTS

1. Reading to build understanding
4. Spoken, written, and visual language for effective communication
6. Application of language structure and conventions to create, critique, and discuss
12. Spoken, written, and visual language to accomplish one's own purposes

MATHEMATICS

1. Numbers and operations
5. Data analysis and probability
6. Problem solving
9. Connections

TECHNOLOGY

1. Basic operations and concepts
4. Technology communications tools

TASK/PROJECT OBJECTIVES

COMPREHENSION OF CONCEPTS	SKILL AND PROCESS DEVELOPMENT

At the end of this project, students will be able to demonstrate comprehension of . . .
  – Why the fraction rules work
  – The reasonability of an answer
	At the end of this project, students will be able to . . .
	  – Estimate products of huge numbers
	  – Apply fraction rules
	  – Calculate probability using "brute force" method
	  – Recognize numerical patterns
	  – Create numerical patterns using recursive functions in Excel

WRITE YOUR OWN TEXTBOOK: CULMINATING TASK ORGANIZER

PRODUCTS AND/OR PERFORMANCES

GROUP PRODUCTS	INDIVIDUAL PRODUCTS	EXTENSIONS
Students will create textbook unit 1.7 (actual book has only 1.1–1.6)	Daily practice writing "Why?" Daily practice estimating answers.	The Bunny Problem (patterns problem) Monty Hall Problem (probability problem)

CRITERIA FOR TASK/PROJECT EVALUATION

GROUP PRODUCTS	INDIVIDUAL PRODUCTS	EXTENSIONS
1. Accuracy (of "How?") 2. Clarity (of "Why?") 3. Appropriateness problem set 4. Appearance	Evidence of improvement in accuracy and reasonability of logic	Students may be awarded extra points for working on extension activities.

WRITE YOUR OWN TEXTBOOK: RUBRIC

Criteria Evaluated	1 Novice Beginning No, Not Yet	2 Basic Developing Yes, But	3 Proficient Accomplished Yes	4 Advanced Exemplary Yes Plus
Accurate explanation of *mechanics* (the "How?" part)	Vague and confusing explanation of how to carry out operation. The sample problem may be correct, but the explanation is not well thought out.	Plausible explanation of how to carry out each operation, but with 2–3 errors, unclear steps, or imprecise language.	Good explanation of how to carry out each operation, with an accurate and appropriate example.	Elegant and concise explanation of how to carry out the operations. Contains no unnecessary words. Includes an appropriate sample problem.
Clear explanation of underlying concept (the "Why?" part)	Demonstrates incomplete understanding of the underlying concept. Sample problem is not appropriate or inaccurate.	Uneven explanation of the underlying theory. Contains good concepts but is not yet a convincing argument.	Good explanation of why the mechanics work, with an appropriate visual or real-world example.	Sophisticated and concise explanation of the underlying theory. Mathematically rigorous, and able to be understood by an inexperienced reader.

(Continued)

	1 Novice Beginning No, Not Yet	2 Basic Developing Yes, But	3 Proficient Accomplished Yes	4 Advanced Exemplary Yes Plus
WRITE YOUR OWN TEXTBOOK: RUBRIC (Continued)				
Criteria Evaluated				
Appropriate problem set	Problem set does not contain appropriate material, and the solutions are inaccurate.	Problem set is mostly appropriate, but contains some questions that are too easy, too hard, or not related to the material. There are a few errors in the solutions.	Problem set includes appropriate examples (and solutions) for each of the basic operations. Problem set includes a question that asks "tell a story related to this operation."	Problem set includes appropriate questions and very thorough answers. Problem set includes a handful of challenge problems that integrate other mathematical material.

3

How to Build
a Better Rubric

Developing a Unit Assessment Plan

PERFORMANCE ASSESSMENT

In recent years, much emphasis has been placed on the ways in which assessment practices are changing. One important outcome from new assessment practices, called "alternative" or "authentic" assessment, is the recognition that comprehension and understanding come as a result of classroom activities. Teachers need to be alert to the risk that even though students are *doing,* they are not necessarily *understanding.*

Interdisciplinary performance assessments are assessments that reflect new learning research because performance tasks, by definition, are integrated and contextualized (tasks created within a real-world context). With such contextual assessments, student products and/or tasks are no longer isolated from outcomes, and content knowledge is no longer fragmented into separated subject areas. Assessment of critical thinking processes, rather than the memorization of bits and pieces of isolated information, is what takes place within the authentic, ambiguous, and messy problems that form the basic assessment structure.

Because the new performance assessment models, such as observations, portfolios, and performance tasks, are so unlike traditional multiple-choice or short-answer tests, they cannot be evaluated in the traditional manner. An alternative assessment methodology is needed to provide a valid as well as an objective basis for evaluation, one that will withstand concerns about the reliability of scores based on human judgment. In an effort to deal with these concerns, new evaluation methodologies have been developed to go along with the new assessments. To be valid, these new tools and methods must be based on clearly articulated standards. A Scoring Rubric is one way of communicating such standards before, during, and after a unit of study.

RUBRICS TO THE RESCUE

Evaluation of an interdisciplinary performance assessment must be based on clearly articulated criteria and performance standards rather than a curve or norm (criteria based rather than norm based). A multifaceted scoring system called a *rubric* (an assessment system in which student work is evaluated according to a set of established criteria rather than the scores of other students) is employed. Rubrics describe the levels of performance a student might be expected to attain relative to a desired standard of achievement. These performance indicators (descriptions) tell the evaluator specifically which characteristics or attributes to look for in a student's work and then where to place that work on a predetermined gradation scale. This type of system encourages student growth by taking the mystery out of success through the use of performance indicators. These indicators allow students to envision and understand what excellence looks like at the outset of the problem task. Performance assessments also encourage introspective intellectual development by making metacognitive activities such as self-assessment and self-reflection part of the total evaluation process. (See Figure 3.1.)

Rubrics provide an excellent means of standards and goals communication because they have the advantage of offering both students and parents the opportunity to understand what learning is taking place in the classroom as well as the content standards included in that learning. By introducing the rubric at the beginning of a unit, teachers let students know from the start exactly what

Figure 3.1   Characteristics of Quality Assessment

Quality Assessment . . .
- ❏ Is flexible enough to allow for individual learner differences
- ❏ Supports ongoing evaluation, providing feedback and opportunities for reteaching during learning
- ❏ Aligns with rigorous curriculum
- ❏ Contains specific delineated benchmarked levels, which illustrate performance expectations via exemplars, samples, and/or models
- ❏ Uses measures that are valid for the individual learner being assessed
- ❏ Is based on high-level content standards
- ❏ Makes metacognitive activities (for example, self-assessment and self-reflection) part of the total evaluation process
- ❏ Is evaluated through clearly articulated criteria
- ❏ Is organic to the context of the learning activity

the expectations for achievement are. Because the rubric describes the specific characteristics contained within each of the performance levels, there are no surprises about the appearance of those expectations at each of the levels or about how those expectations are to be evaluated.

> **Assessment system** refers to an adequate description of a given phenomenon typically requiring more than one piece of relevant information. Test scores may serve as one of many different indicators that comprise a complex system (Sirotnik & Kimball, 1999).

For the teacher, rubrics encourage the determination of performance expectation at levels other than excellent. Rubrics prompt educators to reflect on the validity and value of tasks and activities before they are assigned as well as after they are completed. As essential tools of quality assessment, rubrics also help the teacher visualize the final product's appearance. (See Figures 3.2 and 3.3.)

Design Methodology

The rubric design methodology employed throughout this book is based on the use of clearly delineated standards and a difficulty multiplier. The difficulty multiplier (DM) is based on a concept adapted from one of the Olympic Games scoring modalities used at competitive events such as diving, where it is commonly referred to as the "degree of difficulty." The DM allows the rubric designer to weigh certain evaluation criteria or qualities more or less than others.

> **DIFFICULTY MULTIPLIER**
>
> A scoring modality that allows an evaluator to give variable weight to certain criteria

By using the DM concept, teachers and evaluators are able to differentiate and individualize assessment within the class yet use the same rubric for all students. For example, if a student has a diagnosed learning disability or special need listed on the student's Individual Education Plan (IEP) that calls for spelling to be omitted from the grading component, that student's rubric can be modified so that the criterion of spelling has a difficulty multiplier of 0. The ability to differentiate for students within the same rubric allows the evaluator to use a uniform rubric within a heterogeneous class.

In addition, using the DM concept allows the rubric to be scored in a manner that will result in a grade that is based on a scale of 0 to 100. Each of the criteria to be graded would be assigned a numerical value of 4, 3, 2, or 1

Figure 3.2   Designing Valid and Reliable Nontraditional Assessment

❐ What subject area content and/or process standards are being addressed?

❐ Exactly what should students know and be able to do?

❐ Are the goals and objectives for those content and/or process standards embedded in realistic and worthwhile activities?

❐ Are student activities relevant and meaningful?

❐ Can the evidence of activity completion be quantified or qualified in some way?

❐ What will constitute evidence of student understanding?

Figure 3.3   Design Questions for Creating Performance Assessments

1. Assessment Context and Purpose

   - What is the purpose of the assessment?
   - What, exactly, is being evaluated?
   - What are the content standards or qualities you wish to assess?

2. Assessment Task

   - What is the nature of the task to be done?
   - How does it relate to your unit?
   - What types of student performances are desired and expected?
   - How extensive is it in scope?
   - How authentic is it?

3. Assessment Performance

   - What performance, products, or other evidence will be produced?
   - What will mastery look like?

depending on the quality level of that aspect of the student's work (4 being the highest level and 1 being the lowest). This constitutes the raw score (RS), which is then multiplied by the difficulty multiplier (DM) to produce the final score (FS) for that particular criterion. After each of the criteria has been evaluated in this manner, the resulting sum will constitute the total numerical grade. Please note that in order for this evaluation process to result in a score between 0 and 100, the sum of all the DMs cannot exceed 25. For example, if a student were to receive a perfect score of 100, it would mean that he or she would have received a perfect 4 for each of the qualities being assessed. When a raw score of 4 is multiplied by a series of DMs totaling 25, a total score of 100 is achieved. (See Figure 3.4.)

While this score is not a percentage grade, it does create a grade range that is familiar to students. In other words, if a student earns a 3 in every category (Proficient), the final score is 75, which translates to a grade of B in this situation. Figure 3.5 will guide the evaluator in the scoring of such grades.

PROGRESS ASSESSMENT RUBRIC

By using the Progress Assessment Rubric presented as a guide, teachers and evaluators can develop an assessment plan with metacognitive activities and rubrics to fit in with any or all of the unit lessons. Such performance evaluation relies on the active performance of tasks that can be evaluated through teacher observation and student self-reflection.

Creating Descriptor Levels

A well-designed rubric using evaluation criteria or qualities based on standards from professional organizations such as the National Council of Teachers of English (NCTE), the International Reading Association (IRA), or the National

Figure 3.4   Computing the Score

RAW SCORE	DIFFICULTY MULTIPLIER	FINAL SCORE
1–4	Column Total = 25	RS × DM = FS
Sample Scoring		
3	4	12
4	6	24
2	10	20
3	5	15
		Total Grade = 71

Figure 3.5   Grade Range

Raw Score	1		2		3		4	
	25		50		75		100	
	D 17–33		C 42–58		B 67–79		A 87–96	
	D– 13–16	D+ 34–37	C– 38–41	C+ 59–62	B– 63–66	B+ 80–83	A– 84–87	A+ 97–100

Council of Teachers of Mathematics (NCTM) will withstand criticisms of vagueness and subjectivity. At the same time, such rubrics allow for individual learner differences.

Once evaluation criteria have been selected, the rubric designer must then articulate each of the four descriptor levels in clear and specific terms. A good way to do this is to think of the four levels:

1. Advanced/Exemplary: Yes Plus
2. Proficient/Accomplished: Yes
3. Basic/Developing: Yes, But . . .
4. Novice/Beginning: No, Not Yet

Rubrics for accelerated groups can work well when set up with the descriptors arranged in descending order: advanced, proficient, basic, novice. Setting up the descriptors in this way allows the student to see first what excellence looks like.

Rubrics for average groups (or groups with inclusion students) work best when set up with the novice level first, so as not to discourage those students before they even start.

TEMPLATE FOR PROGRESS ASSESSMENT RUBRIC

Criteria Evaluated	1 Novice Beginning No, Not Yet	2 Basic Developing Yes, But	3 Proficient Accomplished Yes	4 Advanced Exemplary Yes Plus
Problem interpretation	Many inaccuracies in interpretation of problem situations; incorrect use of given information	Interpretation of problem situations usually accurate, but given information may be used incorrectly	Accurate interpretation of problem situations and given information most of the time	Consistently sophisticated and accurate interpretation of problem situations and information
Use of solution strategies and approaches	Strategies or approaches that logically relate to the problems rarely used	Strategies or approaches logically relating to the problems not always used	Appropriate use of strategies and approaches most of the time	Clearly creative and insightful use of strategies and approaches
Accuracy of research and information	Research (informational) errors and basic skills errors common throughout	Some research errors and/or basic skills errors	Small but acceptable number of research or procedural errors	Only rare or insignificant errors in research and/or procedures
Accuracy of problem-solving procedures	Errors in basic problem-solving procedures evident throughout	Some errors in basic problem-solving procedures	Few errors or inaccuracies in problem-solving procedures	Only rare or insignificant errors in problem-solving procedures
Review and check of solutions in problem context	Solutions do not bear any relation to the problem context at all	Solutions seem not to have been evaluated within the problem context	Evidence that solutions were usually reviewed and evaluated within the problem context	Clear evidence that solutions were consistently reviewed, analyzed, and evaluated within the problem context

DESIGNING RUBRICS WITH AND FOR STUDENTS

Be aware that for any given unit, a number of rubrics are needed, including one for each activity and the Culminating Task Rubric. Performance assessments are not just a way of evaluating students but are an integral part of the learning process. Students can benefit by designing rubrics, especially those intended for self-assessment. When fully understood by the student, the rubric constructed to evaluate performance can actually enhance performance and

TEMPLATE FOR LANGUAGE ARTS (NCTE/IRA) STANDARDS RUBRIC

NCTE/IRA Standards Evaluated	1 Novice Beginning No, Not Yet	2 Basic Developing Yes, But	3 Proficient Accomplished Yes	4 Advanced Exemplary Yes Plus	RS*	DM	FS
Adjust spoken, written, and visual language to communicate effectively for different purposes	Consistently poor use of conventions, style, and vocabulary in both written and oral reports	Uneven use of conventions, style, and/or vocabulary in either written or oral report	Satisfactory use of conventions, style, and vocabulary in both written and oral reports	Exemplary, well-developed use of conventions, style, and vocabulary in both written and oral reports		5	
Use a wide range of strategies and writing process elements to communicate with different audiences	Satisfactory use of at least 1 strategy and 1 writing process element in either written or oral report	Satisfactory use of at least 1 strategy and 1 writing process element in both written and oral reports	Satisfactory use of a wide range of strategies and writing process elements for written and oral reports	Advanced use of a wide range of strategies and writing process elements for written and oral reports		5	
Gather, evaluate, and synthesize data for communication of discoveries by generating questions and posing problems	• Team questions highly confusing and ambiguous • Consistently poor evaluation, synthesis, and communication of data and information	• Team questions somewhat confusing • Inconsistent evaluation, synthesis, and communication of data and information	• Team questions well thought out and stated • Clear and satisfactory evaluation, synthesis, and communication of data and information	• Team questions at high levels of insight and understanding • Insightful and well-articulated evaluation, synthesis, and communication of data and information		3	
Use a wide variety of technological and informational resources for the gathering, synthesizing, and communication of information	Weak use of libraries, computer networks, and/or videos	Satisfactory use of at least one of the following: libraries, computer networks, and/or videos	Satisfactory use of libraries, computer networks, and videos for gathering, synthesizing, and communicating information	Sophisticated use of libraries, computer networks, and videos for gathering, synthesizing, and communicating information		3	

(Continued)

allow for metacognition. Another by-product of using a rubric at the beginning of a unit is that students feel that the assessment process is more equitable and they understand better what they have to do to attain a certain performance level. (See the rubric templates in Appendix II: Planning Forms.)

TEMPLATE FOR LANGUAGE ARTS (NCTE/IRA) STANDARDS RUBRIC (Continued)

NCTE/IRA Standards Evaluated	1 Novice Beginning No, Not Yet	2 Basic Developing Yes, But	3 Proficient Accomplished Yes	4 Advanced Exemplary Yes Plus	RS*	DM	FS
Use spoken, written, and visual language to accomplish individual purpose (learning and exchange of information)	Consistently poor use of spoken, written, and visual language during the reflection process (metacognition)	Inconsistent use of spoken, written, and visual language during the reflection process (metacognition)	Satisfactory use of spoken, written, and visual language during the reflection process (metacognition)	Advanced and novel use of spoken, written, and visual language during the reflection process (metacognition)		5	
				Total Grade			

*RS (raw score) refers to total of all initial points achieved. Multiply raw score by difficulty multiplier (DM) for final score (FS).

TEMPLATE FOR MATHEMATICS (NCTM) STANDARDS RUBRIC

NCTM Standards Evaluated	1 Novice Beginning No, Not Yet	2 Basic Developing Yes, But	3 Proficient Accomplished Yes	4 Advanced Exemplary Yes Plus	RS*	DM	FS
Standard 1: Numbers and Operations							
Understanding and representing relationships among numbers	Little understanding or representation of relationships among numbers	Inconsistent understanding and representation of relationships among numbers	Satisfactory level of understanding and representation of relationships among numbers	Advanced level of understanding and representation of relationships among numbers		2	
Understanding how numbers relate to operations	Demonstration of weak knowledge of how numbers relate to operations	Demonstration of developing knowledge of how numbers relate to operations	Demonstration of satisfactory knowledge of how numbers relate to operations	Demonstration of advanced knowledge of how numbers relate to operations		2	

TEMPLATE FOR MATHEMATICS (NCTM) STANDARDS RUBRIC							
NCTM Standards Evaluated	**1** **Novice** Beginning **No, Not Yet**	**2** **Basic** Developing **Yes, But**	**3** **Proficient** Accomplished **Yes**	**4** **Advanced** Exemplary **Yes Plus**	**RS***	**DM**	**FS**
Fluent ability to compute and estimate	Unsatisfactory use of both computation and estimation	Inconsistent use of either computation or estimation	Satisfactory use of computation and estimation	Computation and estimation highly fluent		3	
Standard 5: Data Analysis and Probability							
Formulate questions	Team questions very confusing and ambiguous	Team questions somewhat confusing and not well thoughtout	Team questions clearly stated and well thoughtout	Team questions insightful, original, and creative		2	
Select and use appropriate statistical methods to analyze data	Information collected and organized with inappropriate methodologies	Information collected and organized with flawed and weak methodologies	Information collected and organized with satisfactory methodologies, but accuracy may be slightly flawed	Information collected, organized, and represented with highly appropriate methodologies and total accuracy		3	
Develop and evaluate inferences and predictions based on data	Incomplete development of inferences and/or predictions based on student data or information	Development of only 1 predictable inference based on student data or information	Development of at least 1 insightful inference and/or prediction based on student data or information	Development of several insightful inferences and/or predictions based on student data and/or student information		3	
Standard 6: Problem Solving							
Apply a wide variety of strategies to solve problems	Confusing application and explanation of strategy in project solution	Application and explanation of 1 distinct strategy used in project solution	Application and explanation of 2 distinct strategies used in project solution	Application and explanation of 3 or more distinct strategies used in project solution		3	

(Continued)

	1 **Novice** Beginning No, Not Yet	**2** **Basic** Developing Yes, But	**3** **Proficient** Accomplished Yes	**4** **Advanced** Exemplary Yes Plus	RS*	DM	FS
NCTM Standards Evaluated							
Monitor and reflect on the process of mathematical problem solving	Only 1 team member reflection demonstrates satisfactory level of conceptual understanding.	At least 2 team member reflections demonstrate a satisfactory level of conceptual understanding.	Each individual team member reflection demonstrates satisfactory level of conceptual understanding.	Each individual team member reflection demonstrates thorough understanding of all mathematical concepts covered.		3	
Standard 8: Communication							
Organize and consolidate mathematical thinking	Thinking somewhat organized for the communication of either oral or written report	Thinking somewhat organized for the communication of both oral and written reports	Thinking satisfactorily organized into a coherent method of communication for both oral and written reports	Thinking well consolidated and organized into clearly coherent methods of communication for both oral and written reports		2	
Standard 9: Connections							
Recognize and apply mathematics in contexts outside of mathematics	Neither presentation nor report demonstrates satisfactory integration of mathematical concepts for financial planning and time zone changes.	Either presentation or report demonstrates integration of mathematical concepts for financial planning and time zone changes.	Presentation and report both demonstrate satisfactory integration of mathematical concepts for financial planning and time zone changes.	Presentation and report both demonstrate sophisticated integration of mathematical concepts for financial planning and time zone changes.		2	
				Total Grade			

TEMPLATE FOR MATHEMATICS (NCTM) STANDARDS RUBRIC (Continued)

*RS (raw score) refers to total of all initial points achieved. Multiply raw score by difficulty multiplier (DM) for final score (FS).

SOURCE: Reprinted with permission from *Principles and Standards for School Mathematics*, copyright 2006, by the National Council of Teachers of Mathematics. Standards are listed with permission of the National Council of Teachers of Mathematics (NCTM). NCTM does not endorse the content or validity of these alignments.

TEMPLATE FOR RUBRIC FOR ACCELERATED PROBLEM-BASED INSTRUCTION

Criteria Evaluated	4 Advanced Exemplary Yes Plus	3 Proficient Accomplished Yes	2 Basic Developing Yes, But	1 Novice Beginning No, Not Yet	RS*	DM	FS
Problem comprehension	Consistently formulates sophisticated problems and demonstrates in-depth understanding	Formulates problems and demonstrates understanding	Formulates problems but does not always demonstrate understanding	Rarely formulates problems or demonstrates understanding		5	
Strategy development and application	Consistently develops and applies a wide variety of complex and sophisticated strategies	Proficient at strategy development and application	Consistently develops strategies but does not always apply them correctly	Rarely develops strategies and is unable to apply them correctly		4	
Thinking and reasoning	Masterfully demonstrates a profound level of the kind of thinking and reflecting involved in sophisticated reasoning, conjecturing, exploring, and processing	Adequately demonstrates the thinking and reflecting involved in reasoning	Demonstrates the thinking and reflecting involved in reasoning in at least 2 places in the unit	Does not adequately demonstrate the thinking and reflecting involved in reasoning		5	
Communication of ideas and use of terminology and notation	Highly articulate oral and written communication demonstrate consistently clear and masterful use of appropriate terminology and notation	Both oral and written communication demonstrate clear and consistent use of appropriate terminology and notation	Oral and written communication demonstrate inconsistent use of appropriate terminology and notation	Oral and/or written communication do not demonstrate use of appropriate terminology and/or notation		4	

(Continued)

TEMPLATE FOR RUBRIC FOR ACCELERATED PROBLEM-BASED INSTRUCTION (Continued)

Criteria Evaluated	4 Advanced Exemplary Yes Plus	3 Proficient Accomplished Yes	2 Basic Developing Yes, But	1 Novice Beginning No, Not Yet	RS*	DM	FS
Connections	Concepts within the discipline consistently relate to other subject areas and the real world in an elegant and innovative manner	Concepts within the discipline relate to other subject areas and the real world	Attempts made to relate the discipline to other subject areas and the real world	Little or no attempt made to relate the discipline to other subject areas and the real world		4	
Self-Assessment	Consistently demonstrates an intuitive ability to realistically self-evaluate and self-correct work	Demonstrates the ability to self-evaluate and self-correct work	Attempts made to self-evaluate and self-correct work	Little or no attempt made to self-evaluate or self-correct work		3	
				Total Grade			

*RS (raw score) refers to total of all initial points achieved. Multiply raw score by difficulty multiplier (DM) for final score (FS).

TEMPLATE FOR ADVANCED ASSESSMENT RUBRIC

Criteria Evaluated	4 Advanced Exemplary Yes Plus	3 Proficient Accomplished Yes	2 Basic Developing Yes, But	1 Novice Beginning No, Not Yet	RS*	DM	FS
Speed	Faster than a speeding bullet	With a good tailwind, as fast as a speeding bullet	As fast as a speeding bullet, but only if given a very long head start	Not yet as fast as a speeding bullet		8	
Power	More powerful than a locomotive	As powerful as a locomotive with its engine at half-throttle	As powerful as a locomotive but only if it is having engine trouble	Not yet as powerful as a locomotive		9	

TEMPLATE FOR ADVANCED ASSESSMENT RUBRIC

Criteria Evaluated	4 **Advanced** Exemplary **Yes Plus**	3 **Proficient** Accomplished **Yes**	2 **Basic** Developing **Yes, But**	1 **Novice** Beginning **No, Not Yet**	RS*	DM	FS
Ability to leap	Able to leap tall buildings with a single bound	Able to leap tall buildings with a single bound when wearing an antigravity belt	Able to leap tall buildings in a single bound but only if they are made out of blocks	Not yet able to leap tall buildings with a single bound		8	
				Total Grade			

*RS (raw score) refers to total of all initial points achieved. Multiply raw score by difficulty multiplier (DM) for final score (FS).

TEMPLATE FOR ASSESSMENT RUBRIC FOR INCLUSION CLASSROOMS

Criteria Evaluated	1 **Novice** Beginning **No, Not Yet**	2 **Basic** Developing **Yes, But**	3 **Proficient** Accomplished **Yes**	4 **Advanced** Exemplary **Yes Plus**	RS*	DM	FS
Speed	Can run faster than a speeding turtle	Can get there as fast as a speeding bullet but needs a head start	As fast as a speeding bullet if there is a good tailwind	Faster than a speeding bullet		8	
Power	Needs a jump start	More powerful than an outboard motor but only if given UltraMax fuel	More powerful than an outboard motor	More powerful than a locomotive		9	
Ability to leap	Trips over fences	Able to leap over tall fences if given a running start but must be wearing super shoes	Able to leap over tall fences if given a running start	Able to leap tall buildings with a single bound		8	
				Total Grade			

*RS (raw score) refers to total of all initial points achieved. Multiply raw score by difficulty multiplier (DM) for final score (FS).

CHAPTER THREE	Sample Units

"Ancient Egypt" and "Human Body Travel Guide"

Following are two sample interdisciplinary units. Each unit may be used as is or adjusted to fit the particular needs of your classroom.

ANCIENT EGYPT: CULMINATING TASK ORGANIZER

LESSON AT A GLANCE

CURRICULUM AREA(S): Language Arts, Technology, Mathematics, Science, Social Studies, Visual Arts

GRADE LEVEL(S): 9–10

PROJECT DURATION: 2–3 weeks

RESOURCES/MATERIALS: Rulers, pencils, pictures and/or models of various famous sculptures, drawing paper, Inspiration Software®, word processing software, reference books, scissors, glue, oak tag, construction paper, access to Web sites, including the following:
- British Museum's Ancient Egypt site: http://ancientegypt.co.uk/menu.html
- Mark Millmore's Ancient Egypt site: http://www.eyelid.co.uk/
- Jacques Kinnaer's Ancient Egypt site: http://www.ancient-egypt.org/index.html
- University of Memphis Color Tour of Egypt: http://www.memphis.edu/egypt/egypt.html
- In Memory of Architecture Virtual Study Tour: http://archpropplan.auckland.ac.nz/virtualtour/front.html
- Vitruvio Architecture on the Web: http://www.vitruvio.ch/
- Archpedia (an interactive architectural encyclopedia): http://www.archpedia.com

NOTE: For information on Inspiration Software®, visit http://www.inspiration.com.

TASK/PROJECT DESCRIPTION

Taking the role of architects who have been engaged by representatives from a major theme park, students are to design a model of an Egyptian structure. Each pair of students has the responsibility of designing and constructing a scale model of an authentic Egyptian structure. In addition, each pair will conduct research, which will result in a written report or persuasive letter proving authenticity of their model.

STANDARDS ADDRESSED

LANGUAGE ARTS	MATHEMATICS
4. Spoken, written, and visual language for effective communication 7. Research to generate ideas and questions, and pose problems 8. Technological and information resources to gather and synthesize information and to create and communicate knowledge 11. Participation in literacy communities 12. Spoken, written, and visual language to accomplish one's own purposes	1. Numbers and operations 3. Geometry 4. Measurement
TECHNOLOGY	**SCIENCE**
4. Technology communications tools 5. Technology research tools	A. Science as inquiry

ANCIENT EGYPT: CULMINATING TASK ORGANIZER

SOCIAL STUDIES	VISUAL ARTS
1. Culture 3. People, places, and environments 5. Individuals, groups, and institutions	1. Understanding and applying media, techniques, and processes 4. Understanding the visual arts in relation to history and cultures 6. Making connections between visual arts and other disciplines

TASK/PROJECT OBJECTIVES

COMPREHENSION OF CONCEPTS	SKILL AND PROCESS DEVELOPMENT

At the end of this project, students will be able to demonstrate comprehension of . . .
  – Scale
  – Egyptian structures
  – Data gathering
  – Communication of findings
  – Writing process
  – Research process
	At the end of this project, students will be able to . . .
	  – Build a scale model
	  – Conduct research using the Internet
	  – Use the Internet proficiently
	  – Write an expository or persuasive piece
	  – Identify Egyptian structures

PRODUCTS AND/OR PERFORMANCES

GROUP PRODUCTS	INDIVIDUAL PRODUCTS	EXTENSIONS
– Scale model – Written piece	– Table – Graphic organizer – Reflection	– Costume for Egyptian festival

CRITERIA FOR TASK/PROJECT EVALUATION

GROUP PRODUCTS	INDIVIDUAL PRODUCTS	EXTENSIONS
– Scale accuracy – Model authenticity – Technical quality of writing – Content quality of writing	– Table quality – Graphic organizer quality – Quality of reflection	– Costume authenticity

	1 Novice Beginning No, Not Yet	2 Basic Developing Yes, But	3 Proficient Accomplished Yes	4 Advanced Exemplary Yes Plus	RS*	DM	FS
Criteria Evaluated							

ANCIENT EGYPT: CULMINATING TASK RUBRIC

Scale Model:

Criteria	1	2	3	4	RS*	DM	FS
Measurements	4 or more measurement inaccuracies	1–3 measurement inaccuracies	All measurements are accurate	All measurements are precise and highly accurate		5	
Appearance	No adornment	Shares one quality with original	Appearance matches original in color and detail	Appearance matches original in color and texture, with great attention to detail			
Table of measurements	3 or more measurement inaccuracies	1–2 measurement inaccuracies	All measurements are accurate	All measurements are precise and displayed in color in a computer-generated table		4	
Reflection	• Demonstrates reasoning but with key concepts missing • 4 or more errors in grammar or syntax	• Demonstrates reasoning and conjecturing • 1–3 errors in grammar or syntax	• Demonstrates reasoning and conjecturing in a well-developed paragraph • No errors in grammar or syntax	• Demonstrates sophisticated reasoning and conjecturing in a highly analytical and articulate paragraph • No errors in grammar or syntax		3	
Graphic organizer	Contains 3 main ideas but little or no detail provided	Contains 3 main ideas but supporting details contain some inaccuracies	Contains 3 main ideas supported by sufficient relevant details	Contains 3 sophisticated main ideas supported by numerous relevant details displayed on a computer-generated organizer		3	

	1 **Novice** Beginning **No, Not Yet**	2 **Basic** Developing **Yes, But**	3 **Proficient** Accomplished **Yes**	4 **Advanced** Exemplary **Yes Plus**	RS*	DM	FS
Criteria Evaluated							

ANCIENT EGYPT: CULMINATING TASK RUBRIC

Written Piece

Grammar	4 or more errors in grammar and syntax	1–3 errors in grammar and syntax	No errors in grammar and syntax	Precise and well-planned grammar and syntax		1	
Components	• Work is incomplete, with missing components and minimal organization • There is little or no elaboration	• Work contains an introduction, a conclusion, and 3 developed paragraphs • Main ideas have minimal elaboration	• Work is organized, containing an introduction, a conclusion, and 3 developed paragraphs • Main ideas have sufficient elaboration	• Work is exemplary, containing a novel introduction, a powerful conclusion, and 3 well-developed paragraphs • Main ideas have complex elaboration		2	
Content	No description	Minimal description	Satisfactory description	Exemplary and complex description		2	
				Total Grade			

*RS (raw score) refers to total of all initial points achieved. Multiply raw score by difficulty multiplier (DM) for final score (FS).

ANCIENT EGYPT: UNIT OVERVIEW

UNIT AT A GLANCE

CURRICULUM AREA(S): Language Arts, Science, Mathematics, Technology, Social Studies, Visual Arts and data collection skills

GRADE LEVEL(S): 9–10

PROJECT DURATION: 2–3 weeks

UNIT GOALS AND OBJECTIVES

Students will . . .
- Continue to develop written communication and data collection skills
- Learn about a culture different from their own
- Apply mathematical concepts and skills in ways related to real life
- Navigate the Internet to gather information
- Determine the scale size of classroom objects
- Draw objects to scale
- List components of expository writing
- Apply components to a written project
- Communicate conceptual understanding of purpose, opinion, and reason
- Write a persuasive letter

RESOURCES AND MATERIALS

Rulers, pencils, pictures and/or models of various famous sculptures, drawing paper, Inspiration Software®, word processing software, reference books, scissors, glue, oak tag, construction paper, access to Web sites including the following:
- British Museum's Ancient Egypt site: http://ancientegypt.co.uk/menu.html
- Mark Millmore's Ancient Egypt site: http://www.eyelid.co.uk/
- Jacques Kinnaer's Ancient Egypt site: http://www.ancient-egypt.org/index.html
- University of Memphis Color Tour of Egypt: http://www.memphis.edu/egypt/egypt.html
- In Memory of Architecture Virtual Study Tour: http://archpropplan.auckland.ac.nz/virtualtour/front.html
- Vitruvio Architecture on the Web: http://www.vitruvio.ch/
- Archpedia (an interactive architectural encyclopedia): http://www.archpedia.com

STANDARDS ADDRESSED

LANGUAGE ARTS	MATHEMATICS
4. Spoken, written, and visual language for effective communication 7. Research to generate ideas and questions, and pose problems 8. Technological and information resources to gather and synthesize information and to create and communicate knowledge 11. Participation in literacy communities 12. Spoken, written, and visual language to accomplish one's own purposes	1. Numbers and operations 3. Geometry 4. Measurement
SCIENCE	**TECHNOLOGY**
A. Science as inquiry	4. Technology communications tools 5. Technology research tools

ANCIENT EGYPT: UNIT OVERVIEW

SOCIAL STUDIES	VISUAL ARTS
1. Culture 4. People, places, and environment 5. Individuals, groups, and institutions	1. Understanding and applying media, techniques, and processes 4. Understanding the visual arts in relation to history and cultures 6. Making connections between visual arts and other disciplines
EVALUATION PLAN	**EXTENSIONS**
Teacher and students will use rubrics.	Students will create a costume for an Egyptian festival.

INTERDISCIPLINARY LESSONS

Week 1: Egypt on the Web Objectives: At the end of the lesson, students will be able to . . . – Navigate the Internet for the purpose of gathering information	Week 1 Activities – Observe teacher demonstration of Internet research – Perform Internet research and complete recording sheet – Create their own navigation button
Week 2: Scaling the Pyramids Objectives: At the end of the lesson, students will be able to . . . – Identify scale factors – Determine the scale size of classroom objects – Draw objects to scale	Week 2 Activities – Participate in a whole class demonstration of actual and scale sizes of objects – Participate in a small group or whole class discussion concerning scale size – Participate in a whole class demonstration and discussion of scale drawings – Participate in small group exploration and creation of scale drawings of famous structures – Demonstrate independent reflection detailing new learning
Week 3: Write About It Objectives: At the end of the lesson, students will be able to . . . – Complete a graphic organizer for the purpose of organizing ideas – List components of expository writing – Apply components of expository writing to a written project	Week 3 Activities – Conduct small group research – Create a graphic organizer – Write an expository or persuasive piece – Conduct self-assessment – Describe objects – Locate and apply information – Share with others
Week 4: The Ancient Art of Friendship Objectives: At the end of the lesson, students will be able to . . . – Communicate conceptual understanding of purpose, opinion, and reason – Write a persuasive letter	Week 4 Activities – Write a persuasive letter about friendship qualities – Write a persuasive letter about an Egyptian structure

HUMAN BODY TRAVEL GUIDE: CULMINATING TASK ORGANIZER

CURRICULUM AREA(S): Mathematics, Technology, Science, Language Arts, Visual Arts

GRADE LEVEL(S): 4–5

PROJECT DURATION: 2–3 weeks

RESOURCES/MATERIALS: Computer, colored pencils/markers, glue, clay, science magazines, colored paper

TASK/PROJECT DESCRIPTION

A miniature alien just landed on Earth. He is absolutely fascinated with the human body and wants to take a tour inside a body. What will he see? What will he find there? What does each organ do? In groups of 3–4, students will create a travel guide of their bodies. This guide is to include a map of the inside of the human body and information on what there is to see and do inside the body. They will also list prices for adults, children, seniors, and families. (Students will determine how much percentage off the regular adult price the discounts are.) In addition to their brochure, each person in the group needs to make a mold of an organ that people would see inside their bodies. Finally, students are to create a jingle/song for one or more of the organs that would make people want to visit their body. Weekly journals of progress, group work, and reflection are also required. Projects will be presented to the class.

STANDARDS ADDRESSED

MATHEMATICS	SCIENCE
1. Numbers and operations	A. Science as inquiry C. Life science

TECHNOLOGY	LANGUAGE ARTS
1. Basic operations and concepts 4. Technology communications tools	1. Reading to build understanding 4. Spoken, written, and visual language for effective communication 12. Spoken, written, and visual language to accomplish one's own purposes

VISUAL ARTS

1. Understanding and applying media, techniques, and processes
6. Making connections between visual arts and other disciplines

TASK/PROJECT OBJECTIVES

COMPREHENSION OF CONCEPTS	SKILL AND PROCESS DEVELOPMENT
At the end of this project, students will be able to . . . – Explore how the human body works – Describe the main functions of each organ – Employ different technologies – Map out the organs correctly in the human body – Create a representational model of an organ	At the end of this project, students will be able to . . . – Collect and organize data – Use various sources of information (magazines, Internet, books, articles) to complete tasks – Work in groups and communicate effectively – Brainstorm and produce results collectively – Calculate prices and percentages – Use proofreading and editing skills – Follow directions and time guidelines

HUMAN BODY TRAVEL GUIDE: CULMINATING TASK ORGANIZER

PRODUCTS AND/OR PERFORMANCES

GROUP PRODUCTS	INDIVIDUAL PRODUCTS	EXTENSIONS
– Creation of brochure – Creation of jingle – Map of organs in body – Presentation	– Organ models – Weekly reflective journals – Research journal – Art/pictures	– After the project is completed, have a Human Body Travel Fair in which students would set up their materials in different areas of the room and present the material to children in the lower grades.

CRITERIA FOR TASK/PROJECT EVALUATION

GROUP PRODUCTS	INDIVIDUAL PRODUCTS	EXTENSIONS
– Quality of brochure (accuracy, clarity, creativity, appearance) – Quality of jingle (accuracy, rhythm, memorable) – Body map (accuracy, clarity) – Presentation (organization, knowledge, clarity, visual aids)	– Model of organ (realism, accuracy) – Reflective/progress journals (reflective, knowledge)	– Ask the children in the lower grades what they learned from visiting the human body booths.

HUMAN BODY TRAVEL GUIDE RUBRIC: INDIVIDUAL WORK

Criteria Evaluated	1 Novice Beginning No, Not Yet	2 Basic Developing Yes, But	3 Proficient Accomplished Yes	4 Advanced Exemplary Yes Plus	RS*	DM	FS
Organ Model							
REALISM Is the model a realistic representation of the organ?	The organ is not realistic.	The model has some realistic characteristics of the organ.	The model is a realistic representation of the organ.	The model is an exact replica of the human organ.		3	
ACCURACY Does the model contain the correct elements within each organ?	The model contains only a few accurate elements of the organ.	The model contains some accurate elements of the organ.	The model contains accurate parts of the organ.	The model contains all the exact parts within the organ.		2	
Reflective/Progress Journal							
REFLECTIVE Does the journal reflect the student's thoughts and questions about the subject matter	The journal does not show reflections of the student's thoughts and questions about the subject matter.	The journal presents some reflections of the student's thoughts and questions about the subject matter.	The journal reflects the student's thoughts and questions about the subject matter.	The journal presents an exemplary reflection of the student's thoughts and questions about the subject matter.		2	
KNOWLEDGE Does the journal contain the student's research information obtained from each work session?	The journal does not contain any student research information.	The journal contains a small amount of research information collected from each work session.	The journal contains the student's research information collected from each work session.	The journal contains outstanding knowledge of the subject matter obtained from each work session.		3	
				Total Grade			

*RS (raw score) refers to total of all initial points achieved. Multiply raw score by difficulty multiplier (DM) for final score (FS).

HUMAN BODY TRAVEL GUIDE RUBRIC: GROUP WORK

Criteria Evaluated	1 Novice Beginning No, Not Yet	2 Basic Developing Yes, But	3 Proficient Accomplished Yes	4 Advanced Exemplary Yes Plus	RS*	DM	FS
Brochure Contents							
ACCURACY Is the content material accurate?	Contains numerous inaccuracies	Contains some inaccuracies in information and references	Accurate with some references	Highly accurate, detailed, and with numerous references		3	
CLARITY AND ORGANIZATION Is the material presented clear, organized, and legible?	Confusing, disorganized, and illegible	Somewhat organized but is confusing in places	Clear, organized, and legible	Sophisticated organization, clear articulation, and highly legible		2	
CREATIVITY AND APPEARANCE Is it creative, novel, and one of a kind? Are the pictures colorful and varied?	The brochure is not creative or interesting, and it contains no pictures.	The brochure has some creativity and colorful pictures.	The brochure is novel. Pictures are colorful, varied, and attractive.	The brochure is highly unique and original. Pictures employ innovative use of color and composition.		2	
Jingle Contents							
ACCURATE INFORMATION Is the information in the jingle accurate?	Numerous inaccuracies	Some inaccuracies	Accurate	Accurate and detailed		1	
RHYTHM AND MEMORABLE Does the jingle have rhythm and can it be easily remembered?	• Can't dance to it yet • Hard to remember	• Has a beat • Most words make sense	• Good rhythm • Logical word choice	• Music you can't get out of your head • Catchy words		1	
Body Map							
ACCURACY AND READABILITY Are organs labeled correctly and in the correct place?	Organs not correctly labeled or correctly placed	Most organs correctly labeled and correctly placed	All organs correctly labeled and correctly placed	All organs correctly labeled and placed with a key/legend for clarification		1	

(Continued)

	1 Novice Beginning No, Not Yet	2 Basic Developing Yes, But	3 Proficient Accomplished Yes	4 Advanced Exemplary Yes Plus	RS*	DM	FS
HUMAN BODY TRAVEL GUIDE RUBRIC: GROUP WORK (Continued)							
Criteria Evaluated							
Class Presentation							
KNOWLEDGE Is knowledge of the organs and the human body adequate?	Inadequate knowledge of organs and body	Information on organs and body accurate in places	Adequate information on organs and body	Extensive, detailed, and highly accurate information on organs and body.		2	
CLARITY AND ORGANIZATION Is the presentation clear and organized?	Confusing and disorganized	Makes sense but is disorganized	Clear and organized	Very easy to understand and follow without any effort		2	
VISUAL AIDS Does the group use visual aids (models, map, and so on) in the presentation?	No use of visual aids	Some use of visual aids	Adequate use of visual aids	Sophisticated use of exciting visual aids		1	
				Total Grade			

*RS (raw score) refers to total of all initial points achieved. Multiply raw score by difficulty multiplier (DM) for final score (FS).

HUMAN BODY TRAVEL GUIDE: UNIT PLANNING MAP

UNIT AT A GLANCE	LESSON 1: Organ Search	LESSON 1: PERSPECTIVE
TOPIC: The Human Body CURRICULUM AREA(S): Science, Mathematics, Language Arts, Technology, Visual Arts GRADE LEVEL(S): 4–5 UNIT OBJECTIVES: At the end of the unit, students will be able to . . . – Use the Internet and other sources to gain knowledge – Identify different organs of the human body – Know where in the body each organ is located and understand its function in the human body – Communicate and learn from their peers – Create visual models representing the different organs in the human body TECHNOLOGY: Internet research and word processing programs ASSESSMENT: Rubrics, science journals, teacher observations, research facts, and student's work	OBJECTIVES: Students will be able to . . . – Describe where organs are located in the human body and understand their functions ACTIVITIES: – Create KWL chart on the human body with the class. – In groups, students will create life models of the human body out of rolled paper, and glue organs on the model where they belong. – Students will use different resources (Internet, books, and so on) to find facts about each organ and discover where they belong in the body. – Discuss the facts each group discovered about each organ. – Students will write in science journal.	ENGAGING THE LEARNER: Show students chart of the human body. EXPLORING PRIOR KNOWLEDGE: Create a KWL chart with the class. EXPLORING NEW IDEAS/CONCEPTS: Students will create human body model and use different resources to find out where each organ belongs in the body. ELABORATING ON NEW LEARNING: Discuss what each group discovered about the different organs in the human body. ASSESSING STUDENT UNDERSTANDING: Ask students questions while they do their group projects. Students will create model of the organs in the body. CLOSURE/REFLECTION: Students will display their models in the classroom. The class will have an open discussion about the facts they learned about the organs of the human body. Students will then write a reflection of today's lesson in science journal.
	LESSON 2: The Digestive System	**LESSON 2 PERSPECTIVE**
	OBJECTIVES: Students will be able to . . . – Explain the human digestive system as well as the sizes of the small and large intestines ACTIVITIES: – Students will use an 8-yard and 2-yard piece of string representing the small and large intestines and coil them into a 10-centimeter and a 6-centimeter square. – Students will then coil their string on the models of the human body they created yesterday.	ENGAGING THE LEARNER: Read *The Magic School Bus Inside the Human Body* to the class and discuss. EXPLORING PRIOR KNOWLEDGE: Review what information students know about the organs of the digestive system. EXPLORING NEW IDEAS/CONCEPTS: Students will coil the string around different-sized squares to understand the length of the small and large intestines and how they wind back and forth in the human body.

(Continued)

HUMAN BODY TRAVEL GUIDE: UNIT PLANNING MAP (Continued)

	– Students will record findings on recording sheet. – Students will write in science journal.	ELABORATING ON NEW LEARNING: Students will then coil their string on the models of the human body they created yesterday to visualize exactly how the intestines are in the human body. ASSESSING STUDENT UNDERSTANDING: Ask students questions throughout the lesson. Review each student's recording sheet as well as student's journal. CLOSURE/REFLECTION: At the end of the lesson, the class will have a group discussion about what they learned today about the digestive system and complete their science journals on their own.
	LESSON 3: The Brain	**LESSON 3 PERSPECTIVE**
	OBJECTIVES: Students will be able to . . . – Review and discuss the importance of the human brain ACTIVITIES: – Students will make observations of a sheep's brain and discuss as a class what they see. – Students will weigh different objects representing the size of a baby's, a teen's, and an adult's brain and compare their findings. – Students will create a model of the human brain using the different materials that they are given to make it look like a human brain. – Students will then write a "Brain Recipe" about the materials they used in their model and how they placed them together. – Students will write in science journal.	ENGAGING THE LEARNER: Students will look at a sheep's brain and discuss what they see. EXPLORING PRIOR KNOWLEDGE: Discuss as a class the function of the human brain. Students will also report their findings on the weight of the human brain. EXPLORING NEW IDEAS/CONCEPTS: Students will create a model of the human brain. ELABORATING ON NEW LEARNING: Students will create a "recipe," a how-to guide of their model brain, and share the recipe with the class. ASSESSING STUDENT UNDERSTANDING: Ask questions, review student's written recipe and model brain. CLOSURE/REFLECTION: Students will share their model of the brain with the class and tell why they chose the materials they did to make the brain. As a group, the class will discuss what they learned about the human brain.

HUMAN BODY TRAVEL GUIDE: UNIT PLANNING MAP

LESSON 4: The Lungs	LESSON 4 PERSPECTIVE
OBJECTIVES: Students will be able to . . . – Use a lung model to demonstrate the path oxygen takes through the body ACTIVITIES: – Create a lung model in groups, using a plastic bottle, balloon, rubber band, tape, and a plastic bag. – Use the model to demonstrate the flow of oxygen through the body and record findings. – Match each item in the model to the body part it represents. – Create a map/drawing of the flow of oxygen through the lungs labeling each part. – Students will write in science journal.	ENGAGING THE LEARNER: Discuss the lungs with the whole class. EXPLORING PRIOR KNOWLEDGE: Do breathing exercise to begin lesson on the flow of oxygen through the lungs. EXPLORING NEW IDEAS/CONCEPTS: Students will create lung model and chart the flow of oxygen through the model in groups. ELABORATING ON NEW LEARNING: Students will work individually to create a map/drawing of the flow of oxygen through the lungs. ASSESSING STUDENT UNDERSTANDING: Review students' group model of the lungs as well as individual drawings of the flow of oxygen through the lungs. CLOSURE/REFLECTION: Students will discuss as a group what they have learned about the flow of oxygen through the lungs. They will complete their individual reflections in their science journal.
LESSON 5: The Heart	LESSON 5 PERSPECTIVE
OBJECTIVES: Students will be able to . . . – Describe the path of blood flow through the heart ACTIVITIES: – Discuss pulse with students. Have them find their pulse and calculate the beats per minute when standing and after jogging in place. – Review transparencies of the heart and its sections. Show how the blood flows through the heart. – Have students act out the flow of blood through the heart. – Students will write in science journal.	ENGAGING THE LEARNER: Students will participate in pulse activity, finding the number of times their heart beats per minute when standing and after jogging. EXPLORING PRIOR KNOWLEDGE: Review transparencies as a group. EXPLORING NEW IDEAS/CONCEPTS: Students will act out the flow of blood in groups. ELABORATING ON NEW LEARNING: As a group, students will discuss the flow of blood through the heart. ASSESSING STUDENT UNDERSTANDING: Walk around and ask questions to see if students are understanding the flow of blood. CLOSURE/REFLECTION: Review lesson, and ask for student feedback on the activity. Complete the L part of the KWL chart on what students learned about the human body.

Unit Panorama

Using the Unit Planning Map and the Unit Overview

BRINGING THE BIG PICTURE INTO FOCUS

The purpose of the Unit Planning Map and the Unit Overview is to provide the unit designer with a comprehensive picture of the unit. By using such a panorama, the designer can view the rhythm and flow of the lessons—the sequencing and integration of new information with information already known and understood. Taking a broad view is essential to the facilitation of meaningful learning because new ideas and information must be connected to previously learned concepts within a meaningful context, or they will not become meaningful to the learners.

UNIT DESIGN: ADDRESSING THE MANY FACETS OF MEANING

Planning for meaning requires that one look at the big picture. By using a unit planning tool that focuses attention on the quality and depth of the learning that will take place, teachers can ascertain ahead of time that instruction will be of the highest quality, productive, and enjoyable. Because this learning is relevant, contextual, and meaningful to students, the brain readily processes it so that what is learned can become enduring knowledge rather than isolated bits and pieces of information that are soon forgotten.

An integrated unit plan provides a framework that helps the educator reflect upon and organize change and development within a unit. The Unit

Planning Map and the Unit Overview are the tools educators can use to develop a unit. Inherent in a quality interdisciplinary unit are consideration and attention to the following:

- **Goals and Objectives:** Content and processes to be addressed through the unit
- **Multiple Standards:** Either the framework developed by the state as guidelines in the development and assessment of curricula or national association standards frameworks such as the National Council of Teachers of Mathematics (NCTM) *Principles and Standards for School Mathematics* (2000).
- **Logistics:** The places where the problem-solving activities will take place (the classroom, the computer lab, the library, and so on) and the length of time the students will have to work on the project
- **Tools:** Educational resources, materials, technology required, and so on
- **Tasks:** The research and/or problem activities that students will be asked to perform or solve
- **Interactions:** The ways in which students will work with each other (independently, cooperatively, collaboratively); the ways in which teachers will work with students; the ways in which students will interact with others (for example, interview individuals from other classes)
- **Assessment:** The criteria by which student learning and growth will be evaluated

The checklist in Figure 4.1 can help the teacher focus on meaningful learning and active learner inquiry.

CURRICULAR MODELS

Several organization models can be used to address standards.

- Case studies
- Problem-based learning
- Service learning
- Thematic learning

Case Studies

Case studies employ a narrative that is the basis of the unit. Case studies usually raise a compelling and not easily answered issue that students are to explore. Students investigate the topic's pros and cons and come up with a position that they can defend or a proposed resolution to the issue.

Problem-Based Learning

The work undertaken in problem-based learning (PBL) is closely related to the work in case studies. Here, too, the problem is the force that drives student learning. The more relevant the problem is to the students' reality, the more

Figure 4.1   Checklist for Active Learner Inquiry

❏ Who will be in charge of the learning? Is it to be student centered or teacher centered? Does it promote knowledge-building skills?

❏ Is the inquiry or task structured around primary concepts? For example:
- Big ideas
- Essential questions
- Enduring knowledge (ideas and concepts worth knowing beyond the classroom)
- Individual facts (for example, how does pollution alter habitats?) not factual details (for example,, will fluorocarbon emissions cause environmental change?)

❏ Will students get to express their opinions and points of view, and discuss their analyses?

❏ Do the inquiry questions posed require in-depth research and analysis or a singular response?

❏ Has cognitive terminology (for example, *classify, analyze, predict, create*) been used in framing the task?

❏ Should students include a journal and/or a bibliography as representative of their process?

❏ Should the project include self-assessment (group and/or individual)?

❏ How will students demonstrate their research and learning?

compelling students will find it and the more learning will occur. PBL demands that there be more than one possible solution for the learning to be termed "problem based." Students' final products may indeed offer solutions, but the validity of each solution has a direct correlation to the depth and complexity of the research, analysis, and synthesis of information from which that student's solution was derived.

Sometimes referred to as "inquiry learning," PBL is rooted in human curiosity, which drives the research, analysis, and refinement of the original question. There are few persons who are not excited by such problem-based, inquiry learning; however, it is important to make certain that the inquiry is not only exciting and interesting but also transferable to other contexts and that the inquiry is in alignment with curriculum goals and standards. Among the many advantages of using the Unit Planning Map or the Unit Overview is that its structure prompts the teacher to stop and think about maintaining the connection between goals and enthusiastic inquiry.

Service Learning

Service projects can be undertaken as a means for studying a problem or phenomenon. Service learning often involves working closely with the community outside the classroom or even outside the students' immediate surroundings. Although this model can be a powerful way to make learning meaningful, keep in mind that its validity in the learning process is directly connected to the standards and/or curriculum objectives it is meant to achieve.

Thematic Learning

Themes can be used to cluster content areas and drive instruction. Thematic learning chooses a broad theme, such as *circles.* Circles would then be the entry point to the various content areas. (See Figure 4.2.) Investigation and inquiry are the basis for each of these curricular organizations.

CHOOSING WHICH TOOL TO USE

Each part of the Unit Planning Map and the Unit Overview is essential to successful planning. As outlined in Chapter 1, both the Unit Planning Map and the Unit Overview are means for developing a comprehensive unit design; the

Figure 4.2   Circles Make the World Go 'Round

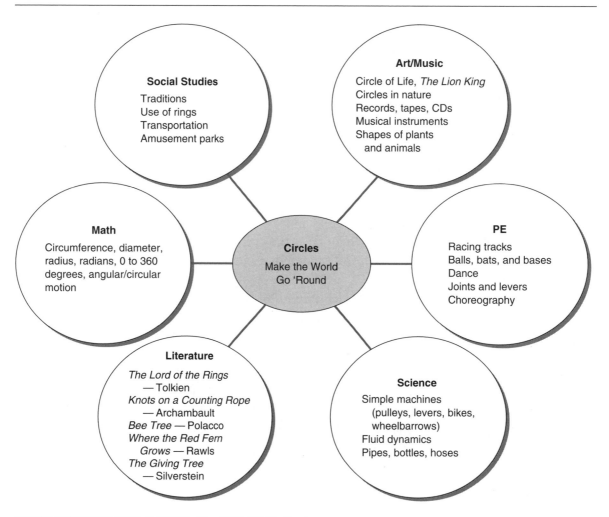

choice of which to use is dependent upon the practitioner and, to a lesser extent, the level at which the unit will be put into action. (See the descriptive templates for the Unit Planning Map and the Unit Overview in Chapter 1.) Each tool draws on decisions made about the unit while the Culminating Task was being developed. Figure 4.3 shows the common aspects of the Unit Planning Map and the Unit Overview.

Resources and Materials

Both the Unit Planning Map and the Unit Overview feature a Resources and Materials section. You'll find that the materials you select to use can have a dramatic impact on the potential success of a unit. The resources must be appropriate to the level and broad enough for students to draw their own conclusions. Tools that allow for student inquiry include the following:

- Electronic resources (DVDs and Web sites)
- Print reference and research material
- Access to facilities, such as technology or science labs
- Human resources (people who could be used as either audiences or sources of information)

Because motivation has a dramatic effect on student achievement, the materials used should sustain the interest and excitement generated by the Culminating Task project. Interacting with technology is exciting for students.

Figure 4.3   Common Aspects of the Unit Planning Map and Unit Overview

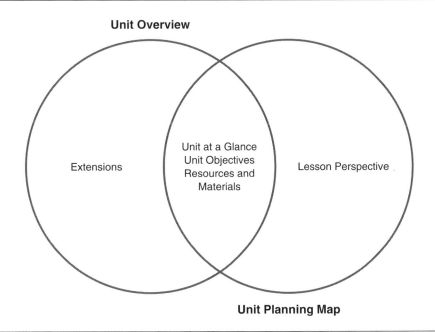

Figure 4.4   Internet Resource Sites

To Connect With Colleagues

Apple Learning Interchange
    http://www.apple.com/education/community/ali.html
Association for Supervision and Curriculum Development
    http://www.ascd.org

To Develop Insight Into the Nature of Content Disciplines

The Center for Arts Education
    http://www.cae-nyc.org
The Getty
    http://www.getty.edu/education
MATHCOUNTS
    http://mathcounts.org
Math Forum
    http://mathforum.org
National Geographic Education Guide
    http://www.nationalgeographic.com/education
The World Bank Group's Development Education Program
    http://www.worldbank.org/depweb
World Resources Institute
    http://www.wri.org

To Explore Authentic Audiences for Student Performances and Products

Click to Meet™
    http://www.radvision.com/Products/Desktop
NetMeeting
    http://www.microsoft.com/windows/netmeeting

For Inquiry-Based Learning and Problem Solving

Classroom Connect®
    http://www.classroomconnect.com
The Educator's Reference Desk
    http://www.eduref.org
ERIC—Education Resources Information Center
    http://www.eric.ed.gov
The Global Schoolhouse
    http://www.gsh.org
Institute for Inquiry® (Exploratorium®)
    http://www.exploratorium.edu/ifi
International Society for Technology in Education
    http://www.iste.org
The JASON Project
    http://www.jasonproject.org
Journey North
    http://www.learner.org/jnorth
Problem-Based Learning Network (IMSA)
    http://www2.imsa.edu/programs/pbln
SchoolWorld®
    http://www.schoolworld.com
Smithsonian Education
    http://smithsonianeducation.org/educators/index.html

Many Web sites can help teachers find appropriate resources to increase student motivation and keep the learning experience meaningful and cohesive. See Figure 4.4 for a list of Web sites to visit.

The Unit Planning Map

The Unit Planning Map differs from the Unit Overview in the specificity with which it treats lesson planning. Teachers just entering the profession often find lesson planning one of the most challenging aspects of their jobs. Unit planning can be even more daunting because it requires a vision beyond today's lesson toward outcomes based on state and content area standards as well as district scope and sequence documents. The Unit Planning Map brings the basics of lesson planning to the design of the unit in the Lesson Perspective section. (See the blank Unit Planning Map template in Appendix II: Planning Forms.)

The Lesson Perspective

The Lesson Perspective section of the Unit Planning Map provides a framework and sequence for applying best practice to unit design. This section, which focuses on instructional delivery, addresses students' prior knowledge, promoting high-level thinking, employing authentic assessment, and facilitating transfer through metacognition. Information developed using this section of the Unit Planning Map tool becomes the basis for the Steps and Procedures section of the Interdisciplinary Lesson Plan template. The Lesson Perspective section includes the following prompts:

- Engaging the learner
- Exploring prior knowledge
- Exploring new ideas and concepts
- Elaborating on new learning
- Assessing student understanding
- Closure and reflection

See Chapter 5 for an in-depth discussion of the phases of the Lesson Perspective section of the Unit Planning Map.

The Unit Overview

The Unit Overview is intended for use by teachers who have developed their practice and pedagogy to the extent that they are comfortable with and confident in their lesson planning. However, teachers should choose the tool that works best for them and their classroom circumstances, making modifications to the design as they refine their practice. Even those who seem to have been born to teach reach pedagogical excellence by standing firmly upon their preparation and planning. Simply put, a well-thought-out, comprehensive instructional plan is the basis of good teaching. (See the blank Unit Overview template in Appendix II: Planning Forms.)

Reduced versions of the Unit Planning Map and the Unit Overview appear as Figure 4.5.

PLANNING FOR SUCCESS

Although flexibility and the ability to think on one's feet are certainly high on the list of characteristics of effective teachers, even the best of us cannot plan instruction on the fly, nor can standards be addressed in this way. An instrument such as the Unit Planning Map or the Unit Overview enables teachers to round up the sometimes seemingly disparate elements of modern-day education.

Figure 4.5A   Unit Planning Map and Unit Overview

UNIT PLANNING MAP		
UNIT AT A GLANCE *Foundation of the unit*	**LESSON 1**	**LESSON 1 PERSPECTIVE**
TOPIC: CURRICULUM AREA(S): GRADE LEVEL(S): PROJECT DURATION: UNIT OBJECTIVES: Targets the unit's main purpose TECHNOLOGY: Innovative ways technology can be used to enhance student understanding and stimulate interest ASSESSMENT: • *Means and opportunity for students to "show what they know"* • *Criteria for excellence known to all parties before undertaking an activity, task, or lesson* • *Select and use a variety of assessment techniques (for example, if process, problem-solving, and higher cognitive levels of thinking are emphasized, be sure the assessments clearly reflect those criteria)* RESOURCES AND MATERIALS: Any materials or tools that could be appropriately used for inquiry, but not limited to electronic and print reference materials, access to facilities such as tech or science labs, and human resources, such as persons to interview or to whom students can present.	OBJECTIVES *Specific and measurable concepts to be learned—not the activities students perform to learn:* • *Specific skills, knowledge, and processes* • *Emphasized during instruction* • *Identified beforehand* • *Appropriate assessment techniques must be chosen for the assessment procedures* ACTIVITIES	• *Attends specifically to good pedagogy by focusing on students' prior knowledge, promoting high-level thinking, employing authentic assessment, and facilitating transfer through metacognition* • *Each element of the lesson perspective phrased in terms of what the student will do or learn (The information in the lesson perspective here is carried over to the Steps and Procedures of the Interdisciplinary Lesson Plan.)* ENGAGING THE LEARNER: EXPLORING PRIOR KNOWLEDGE: EXPLORING NEW IDEAS/ CONCEPTS: ELABORATING ON NEW LEARNING: ASSESSING STUDENT UNDERSTANDING: CLOSURE/REFLECTION:
	LESSON 2	**LESSON 2 PERSPECTIVE**
	OBJECTIVES ACTIVITIES	ENGAGING THE LEARNER: EXPLORING PRIOR KNOWLEDGE: EXPLORING NEW IDEAS/ CONCEPTS: ELABORATING ON NEW LEARNING: ASSESSING STUDENT UNDERSTANDING: CLOSURE/REFLECTION:
	LESSON 3	**LESSON 3 PERSPECTIVE**
	OBJECTIVES ACTIVITIES	ENGAGING THE LEARNER: EXPLORING PRIOR KNOWLEDGE: EXPLORING NEW IDEAS/ CONCEPTS: ELABORATING ON NEW LEARNING: ASSESSING STUDENT UNDERSTANDING: CLOSURE/REFLECTION:

UNIT PLANNING MAP		
	LESSON 4	**LESSON 4 PERSPECTIVE**
	OBJECTIVES ACTIVITIES	ENGAGING THE LEARNER: EXPLORING PRIOR KNOWLEDGE: EXPLORING NEW IDEAS/ CONCEPTS: ELABORATING ON NEW LEARNING: ASSESSING STUDENT UNDERSTANDING: CLOSURE/REFLECTION:
	LESSON 5	**LESSON 5 PERSPECTIVE**
	OBJECTIVES ACTIVITIES	ENGAGING THE LEARNER: EXPLORING PRIOR KNOWLEDGE: EXPLORING NEW IDEAS/ CONCEPTS: ELABORATING ON NEW LEARNING: ASSESSING STUDENT UNDERSTANDING: CLOSURE/REFLECTION:
	LESSON 6	**LESSON 6 PERSPECTIVE**
	OBJECTIVES ACTIVITIES	ENGAGING THE LEARNER: EXPLORING PRIOR KNOWLEDGE: EXPLORING NEW IDEAS/ CONCEPTS: ELABORATING ON NEW LEARNING: ASSESSING STUDENT UNDERSTANDING: CLOSURE/REFLECTION:

Figure 4.5B   Unit Planning Map and Unit Overview

UNIT OVERVIEW	
UNIT AT A GLANCE	
CURRICULUM AREA(S):	
GRADE LEVEL(S):	
Foundation of the unit (same as the Unit Planning Map)	
Students will . . .	
UNIT GOALS AND OBJECTIVES	
Objectives phrased as "Students will . . ." and naturally evolve from the unit designer's understanding of the nature of the integrated content and the established standards associated with that content	

RESOURCES AND MATERIALS	
Any tool that could be appropriately used for inquiry, including but not limited to electronic and print reference material, access to facilities such as tech or science labs, and human resources such as persons to interview or to whom students can present	

STANDARDS ADDRESSED	
• *Standards reflected in the objectives* • *Fuel for integration of instruction*	
LANGUAGE ARTS	**MATHEMATICS**
SCIENCE	**TECHNOLOGY**
SOCIAL STUDIES	**VISUAL ARTS**
EVALUATION PLAN	**EXTENSIONS**
• *Keep feedback on learning objectives in mind throughout the unit.* • *Establish what excellence looks like and use it as a basis for developing rubrics that will be used to assess student understanding of each objective.*	• *Activities support transfer of knowledge and promote student metacognition.*

INTERDISCIPLINARY LESSONS	
Week 1: Objectives: • *Phrased in terms of "At the end of the lesson, the student will be able to . . ."* • *Derived from the standards addressed* • *Measurable with some form of authentic assessment*	Week 1 Activities *Inquiry based and designed to meet the weekly unit objectives*
Week 2: Objectives: • *Phrased in terms of "At the end of the lesson, the student will be able to . . ."* • *Derived from the standards addressed* • *Measurable with some form of authentic assessment*	Week 2 Activities *Inquiry based and designed to meet the weekly unit objectives*

UNIT OVERVIEW	
Week 3: Objectives: • *Phrased in terms of "At the end of the lesson, the student will be able to. . . "* • *Derived from the standards addressed* • *Measurable with some form of authentic assessment*	Week 3 Activities *Inquiry based and designed to meet the weekly unit objectives*
Week 4: Objectives: • *Phrased in terms of "At the end of the lesson, the student will be able to. . . "* • *Derived from the standards addressed* • *Measurable with some form of authentic assessment*	Week 4 Activities *Inquiry based and designed to meet the weekly unit objectives*

"A Trip to Outer Space"

Following is a sample interdisciplinary unit. This unit may be used as is or adjusted to fit the particular needs of your classroom.

A TRIP TO OUTER SPACE: CULMINATING TASK ORGANIZER
LESSON AT A GLANCE

CURRICULUM AREA(S): Language Arts, Social Studies, Science, Mathematics
GRADE LEVEL(S): 4
PROJECT DURATION: 5–6 weeks
RESOURCES/MATERIALS:
    – The Earth, Sun, Moon, and Stars Unit (Planets Too!): An Educator's Reference Desk Lesson Plan: http://www.eduref.org/cgi-bin/printlessons.cgi/Virtual/Lessons/Science/Space_Sciences/SPA0007.html
    – The Nine Planets: A Multimedia Tour of the Solar System: http://seds.lpl.arizona.edu/nineplanets/nineplanets/nineplanets.html
    – *The Planets* by Cynthia Pratt Nicolson
    – *Stars & Planets* by David Levy

TASK/PROJECT DESCRIPTION
– Students will work in groups of 3 or 4 as the crew for a fictional space mission. They will operate under the premise that technology has reached the stage where fuel and the time it takes to travel great distances are no longer issues. – Each crew will choose a destination somewhere in our solar system and put together a presentation based on guiding questions. Students will also speculate on the feasibility of establishing either a research station or a space colony on the place they visit, citing what conditions may be favorable for human beings to establish some sort of livable environment, as well as what conditions would be obstacles for long-term inhabitancy. – Group reports will be presented during press conferences for astronauts after they have completed their missions. Prior to the press conference, each group will build a model rocket to symbolize their spaceship. – Students should provide props to use during the press conference—for example, photographs of the crew landed; samples from the place they visited, such as rocks (possibly made of papier-mâché) and soil; and so on. Students may also want to adopt a uniform look for the press conference, which will be videotaped by the instructor. – Students will also hand in a previously prepared written version of their press conference, which will cite sources used.

STANDARDS ADDRESSED

LANGUAGE ARTS	SCIENCE
1. Reading to build understanding 4. Spoken, written, and visual language for effective communication 6. Application of language structure and conventions to create, critique, and discuss 7. Research to generate ideas and questions, and pose problems 8. Technological and information resources to gather and synthesize information and to create and communicate knowledge	A. Science as inquiry B. Physical science D. Earth and space science F. Science in personal and social perspectives

A TRIP TO OUTER SPACE: CULMINATING TASK ORGANIZER

SOCIAL STUDIES	MATHEMATICS
3. People, places, and environments 8. Science, technology, and society	4. Measurement

TASK/PROJECT OBJECTIVES	
COMPREHENSION OF CONCEPTS	**SKILL AND PROCESS DEVELOPMENT**
At the end of this project, students will be able to . . . – Compare and contrast aspects of life here on Earth with conditions on other planets or conditions on or in other objects within our solar system – Describe ways to overcome obstacles to establishing places to live elsewhere in our solar system	At the end of this project, students will be able to . . . – Research and interpret information about other planets or other objects in our solar system – Work as a team to divide up responsibilities and then assemble all the separate portions into an integrated, whole unit for presentation

PRODUCTS AND/OR PERFORMANCES		
GROUP PRODUCTS	**INDIVIDUAL PRODUCTS**	**EXTENSIONS**
– Rocket that will be launched prior to the group's press conference – Props created for use during the press conference – Written report that details information to be presented during the press conference – Videotape of the press conference	Journal entry (or entries) reflecting on the following: – What the student learned about working as a group and possibly comparing that with the need for astronauts to work cooperatively when in outer space – What the student learned about other planets/places visited by the various groups – Any further thoughts about the possibility of human survival elsewhere in our solar system (based on either the student's group research or presentations by other groups)	– Students should complete a final journal reflection on what they learned from the various activities in this unit. – The teacher should encourage students to read more about our solar system and the various people who have traveled in space.

(Continued)

A TRIP TO OUTER SPACE: CULMINATING TASK ORGANIZER (Continued)

CRITERIA FOR TASK/PROJECT EVALUATION

GROUP PRODUCTS	INDIVIDUAL PRODUCTS	EXTENSIONS
– Teacher observation of group cooperation – Rubric to evaluate the following: • Group Report, Part 1: Basic Information About Your Destination*	– Teacher observation – Evaluation of journal entry (or entries) for questions addressed and overall clarity of answers – Discussions with individual students as needed	– Students share journal entries with others for feedback. – Students share knowledge acquired from reading.

CRITERIA FOR TASK/PROJECT EVALUATION

GROUP PRODUCTS	INDIVIDUAL PRODUCTS	EXTENSIONS
• Group Report, Part 2: Comparisons Between Your Destination and Earth* • Group Report, Part 3: Challenge Questions* • Hypothesis on Human Survival Elsewhere in Our Solar System • Presentation of Group Report: Props Used During Press Conference • Presentation of Group Report: Conduct of Members During Press Conference – Group Cooperation During Unit – Clarity and accuracy of information presented during press conference and in written group report (if information is incorrect, work with students to determine whether the sources used were outdated or erroneous)		

* See Facts-to-Find on pages 88–89.

A TRIP TO OUTER SPACE: CULMINATING TASK RUBRIC							
Criteria Evaluated	**1** **Novice** Beginning **No, Not Yet**	**2** **Basic** Developing **Yes, But**	**3** **Proficient** Accomplished **Yes**	**4** **Advanced** Exemplary **Yes Plus**	**RS***	**DM**	**FS**
Group report, Part I: Basic information about your destination	Group report did not provide even partially detailed answers to the minimum of 2 sets of questions listed on the Facts-to-Find sheet.	Group report provided detailed answers to 3 sets of questions listed on the Facts-to-Find sheet.	Group report provided well-written and detailed answers to 4 sets of questions listed on the Facts-to-Find sheet.	Group report provided perceptive, powerfully written, highly accurate, and profoundly detailed answers to more than 4 sets of questions listed on the Facts-to-Find sheet.		4	
Group report, Part 2: Comparisons between your destination and Earth	Group report did not provide even partially detailed, accurate comparisons to the minimum of 2 sets of questions listed on the Facts-to-Find sheet.	Group report provided detailed, correct comparisons to 2–3 sets of questions listed on the Facts-to-Find sheet.	Group report provided well-written and detailed, correct comparisons for 4 sets of questions listed on the Facts-to-Find sheet.	Group report provided perceptive, powerfully written, highly accurate, and profoundly detailed answers to more than 4 sets of questions listed on the Facts-to-Find sheet.		6	
Group report, Part 3: Challenge questions	Group report provided answers that were either inappropriate or inaccurate.	Group report provided acceptable answers to 1 set of challenge questions listed on the Facts-to-Find sheet.	Group report provided well-written, detailed answers to 1 set of challenge questions listed on the Facts-to-Find sheet.	Group report provided perceptive, powerfully written, highly accurate, and profoundly detailed answers to more than 1 set of challenge questions listed on the Facts-to-Find sheet.		5	

(Continued)

A TRIP TO OUTER SPACE: CULMINATING TASK RUBRIC (Continued)

Criteria Evaluated	1 Novice Beginning No, Not Yet	2 Basic Developing Yes, But	3 Proficient Accomplished Yes	4 Advanced Exemplary Yes Plus	RS*	DM	FS
Hypothesis on human survival criteria	Group did not make a reasonable attempt to speculate on human survival criteria.	Group made an attempt to speculate on human survival criteria but did not provide well-thought-out reasons for any of the conditions listed.	Group made 1 reasonable speculation regarding human survival criteria and provided well-thought-out reasons to support the hypothesis.	Group made several perceptive speculations regarding human survival criteria and provided well-thought-out, detailed reasons to support 2 of the conditions speculated.		3	
Presentation of group report: Props used during press conference	Group did not provide any props to enhance press conference presentation, or props used were not appropriate.	Group provided 1–2 appropriate props for the press conference that were connected with and enhanced the presentation.	Group provided 3–4 appropriate props for the press conference that were logically connected with and enhanced the presentation.	Group provided more than 4 inventive props for the press conference that were directly related to and enhanced the presentation.		2	
Presentation of group report: Conduct of members during press conference	• Group members rarely established eye contact with audience. • Group was not expressive and did not make a noticeable effort to behave appropriately during most of the press conference	• Group members made eye contact briefly with audience. • Group was rarely expressive and made some effort to behave appropriately during press conference.	• Group members made good eye contact with audience. • Group was relatively expressive and behaved appropriately during most of the press conference.	• Group members established continuous eye contact with audience. • Group was expressive and behaved appropriately (that is, members were serious, were enthusiastic, or expressed other reactions at appropriate times) during the press conference		3	

A TRIP TO OUTER SPACE: CULMINATING TASK RUBRIC							
Criteria Evaluated	1 **Novice** Beginning **No, Not Yet**	2 **Basic** Developing **Yes, But**	3 **Proficient** Accomplished **Yes**	4 **Advanced** Exemplary **Yes Plus**	RS*	DM	FS
	• Group members not presenting caused unnecessary distractions during presentation	• Group members usually avoided distractions while others were talking.	• Group members did not cause unnecessary distractions.	• Group members not presenting supported the presenters in a subtle way (for example, positive facial expressions)			
Group cooperation during unit	• More than 1 group member was unable to work with other members of the group. • No attempts were made to find a solution or to inform the instructor of problems the group encountered	• 1 group member was unable to work well with others. • Few attempts were made by others in the group to find a solution to resolve team differences.	• Members usually worked well together and were able to complete the work in time for the group presentation. • Members were able to find solutions to problems the group encountered with little teacher intervention	• Members displayed a high level of maturity, working synergistically at all times, and were always able to resolve differences without teacher intervention		2	
				Total Grade			

*RS (raw score) refers to total of all initial points achieved. Multiply raw score by difficulty multiplier (DM) for final score (FS).

A TRIP TO OUTER SPACE: SOCIAL STUDIES STANDARDS (NCSS) RUBRIC

NCSS Standards Evaluated	1 Novice Beginning No, Not Yet	2 Basic Developing Yes, But	3 Proficient Accomplished Yes	4 Advanced Exemplary Yes Plus	RS*	DM	FS
Interpret, use, and distinguish various representations of the Earth, such as maps, globes, and photographs	Weak use of maps and/or photographs throughout both the report and the presentation	Inconsistent quality of map and/ or photograph integration throughout both the report and the presentation	Satisfactory integration of maps and photographs throughout both the report and the presentation	Advanced and thorough integration of maps and photographs throughout both the report and the presentation		2	
Use appropriate resources, data sources, and geographic tools, such as atlases, databases, grid systems, charts, graphs, and maps, to generate, manipulate, and interpret information	Weak use of databases, grid systems, charts, graphs, and maps, resulting in numerous research interpretation flaws	Weak use of databases, grid systems, charts, graphs, and maps, resulting in inconsistent interpretation of research and information	Acceptable interpretation of research and other information developed through use of databases, grid systems, charts, graphs, and maps	Sophisticated interpretations of research and other information developed through extensive use of databases, grid systems, charts, graphs, and maps		3	
Estimate distance and calculate scale	Numerous errors found in distance estimations and map scale calculations (more than 6 errors)	Moderate degree of mathematical error found in distance estimations and map scale calculations (4–6 errors)	Consistently low level of mathematical error found in distance estimations or map scale calculations (2–3 errors)	Highly accurate use of mathematical calculations in the estima-tion of dis-tances and the calculation of map scales employed throughout unit		5	

A TRIP TO OUTER SPACE: SOCIAL STUDIES STANDARDS (NCSS) RUBRIC

NCSS Standards Evaluated	1 Novice Beginning No, Not Yet	2 Basic Developing Yes, But	3 Proficient Accomplished Yes	4 Advanced Exemplary Yes Plus	RS*	DM	FS
Describe and speculate about physical system changes, such as seasons, climate and weather, and the water cycle	Weak knowledge level demonstrated throughout all project aspects dealing with weather and climate	Inconsistent knowledge level demonstrated in all project aspects dealing with weather and climate	Proficient knowledge level demonstrated in all project aspects dealing with weather and climate	Consistently advanced and sophisticated knowledge level demonstrated in all project aspects dealing with weather and climate		4	
Examine the interaction of human beings and their physical environment, the use of land, the building of cities, and ecosystem changes in selected locales and regions	Report and presentation demonstrate extremely poor understanding of how people interact with their environment.	Report and presentation demonstrate inconsistent understanding of how people interact with their environment.	Report and presentation demonstrate satisfactory understanding of how people interact with their environment.	Report and presentation demonstrate numerous examples of astute observation and sophisticated knowledge regarding ways in which people interact with their environment.		6	
				Total Grade			

*RS (raw score) refers to total of all initial points achieved. Multiply raw score by difficulty multiplier (DM) for final score (FS).

A TRIP TO OUTER SPACE: UNIT OVERVIEW

UNIT AT A GLANCE

CURRICULUM AREA(S): Language Arts, Science, Mathematics, Technology, Social Studies

GRADE LEVEL(S): 4

PROJECT DURATION: 6 weeks

UNIT GOALS AND OBJECTIVES

Students will . . .

- Gain a better understanding of how their daily lives are affected by space technology and what is happening in our solar system
- Realize how vast the universe is and how much of it is still hidden from us here on Earth

RESOURCES AND MATERIALS

- Bringing the Solar System to Life: An Educator's Reference Desk Lesson Plan: http://www.eduref.org/cgi-bin/printlessons.cgi/Virtual/Lessons/Science/Astronomy/AST0003.html
- The Earth, Sun, Moon, and Stars Unit (Planets Too!): An Educator's Reference Desk Lesson Plan: http://www.eduref.org/cgi-bin/printlessons.cgi/Virtual/Lessons/Science/Space_Sciences/SPA0007.html
- *Exploring Outer Space: Rockets, Probes, and Satellites* by Isaac Asimov and Francis Reddy
- The Nine Planets: A Multimedia Tour of the Solar System: http://seds.lpl.arizona.edu/nineplanets/nineplanets/nineplanets.html
- *The Planets* by Cynthia Pratt Nicolson
- *Stars & Planets* by David Levy

STANDARDS ADDRESSED

LANGUAGE ARTS	MATHEMATICS
1. Reading to build understanding 4. Spoken, written, and visual language for effective communication 6. Application of language structure and conventions to create, critique, and discuss 7. Research to generate ideas and questions, and pose problems 8. Technological and information resources to gather and synthesize information and to create and communicate knowledge 12. Spoken, written, and visual language to accomplish one's own purposes	1. Numbers and operations 4. Measurement

SCIENCE	TECHNOLOGY
A. Science as inquiry D. Earth and space science	4. Technology communications tools 5. Technology research tools

SOCIAL STUDIES
3. People, places, and environments 8. Science, technology, and society

A TRIP TO OUTER SPACE: UNIT OVERVIEW

EVALUATION PLAN	EXTENSIONS
Assessment will be made through the use of instructor observations, student feedback (either in journal entries or by direct interviews with the instructor), and rubrics.	– A field trip to a local television station to see how satellite technology is used – A field trip to a local planetarium or space museum

INTERDISCIPLINARY LESSONS

Week 1: Introducing the Planets Objectives: At the end of the lesson, students will be able to . . . – Name the planets in our solar system – Place the planets in proper sequential order, beginning with the planet that is closest to the Sun and ending with the planet that is (usually) the farthest away from the Sun – Define *rotation* and *revolution* in relation to the planets	Week 1 Activities – The instructor will take the class to a large field or gym to have them act out the parts of the planets and our Sun. – The instructor will ask students to name the planets in our solar system. – The instructor will select students to represent the Sun and each of the planets. – The instructor will discuss the concept of planets revolving around our Sun and have students practice revolving around the Sun.
Week 2: How Big and How Far? Objectives: At the end of the lesson, students will be able to . . . – Demonstrate the understanding that not all planets are the same size – Approximate distances between the planets and the Sun in our solar system – Demonstrate knowledge of the composition, structures, processes, and interactions of Earth and other planets in our solar system	Week 2 Activities – Students will demonstrate knowledge of each planet's size by choosing correctly from an assortment of fruits and vegetables representing approximate size relationships among the planets.
Week 3: Take Me to Your Leader Objectives: At the end of the lesson, students will be able to . . . – Conduct objective research – List the various physical characteristics of Earth Compare and contrast Earth with other planets or physical objects in our solar system	Week 3 Activities – Students will choose from a list of various questions and research specific facts about Earth. They will use the information they find to write a report of their encounter with an alien being who is visiting Earth and who has chosen that student to be its first contact.
Week 4: 'Round and 'Round They Go Objectives: At the end of the lesson, students will be able to . . . – Explain what makes a satellite a satellite – Differentiate between naturally occurring and man-made satellites – Identify different types of man-made satellites and their uses	Week 4 Activities – After discussing the uses of artificial satellites and the impact they have on our daily lives, students will work in small groups to create models of any type of man-made satellite for display in the classroom. Students will include hangtags giving details about what type of orbit it makes around Earth (and its possible location), as well as any other relevant information.

A TRIP TO OUTER SPACE: FACTS-TO-FIND

Part I—Basic Information About Your Destination

Provide well-written and detailed answers to a minimum of two of the following sets of questions:
- Where did you travel to? For whom or what was the place you traveled to named?
- Who (if anyone) is credited with discovering the place you traveled to, and when was it discovered?
- How old is the place you traveled to?
- What is the surface of the place you traveled to made of? What are some of its known features?
- What is under the surface of the place you traveled to?
- Where is the highest known point on the place you traveled to, and how is it referred to by scientists? (If the highest point does not have a name, do scientists use coordinates when referring to this point?)
- Where is the deepest known point on the place you traveled to, and how is it referred to by scientists? (If the deepest point does not have a name, do scientists use coordinates when referring to this point?)
- If the place you traveled to is a planet, does it have any moons? Does it have any rings?
- If the place you traveled to is not a planet, is it a satellite of a planet? If so, which planet is it a satellite of?

Part II—Comparisons With Earth

Provide well-written and detailed answers to a minimum of two of the following sets of questions:
- What is the diameter of the place you traveled to? How does that compare with the diameter of the planet Earth?
- What is the atmosphere of the place you traveled to made up of? How does that compare to Earth's atmosphere?
- How does the force of gravity on the place you traveled to compare to the force of gravity here on Earth?
- How cold is the coldest spot on the place you traveled to? How does that compare with the coldest place here on Earth?
- How warm is the hottest spot on the place you traveled to? How does that compare to the hottest place here on Earth?
- Does the place you taveled to rotate on an axis? If so, how long does it take to make a complete rotation on its axis? How does that compare with the length of time it takes for Earth to make one complete rotation on its axis?
- If the place you traveled to rotates on an axis, how fast does it rotate when the speed is measured at that place's equator? How does that compare with how fast Earth rotates when its speed is measured at the equator?
- If you traveled to another planet, how long does it take for your planet to make one complete revolution around the Sun? How does that compare with the length of time it takes for Earth to make one complete revolution around the Sun?
- If you traveled to a satellite of another planet, how long does it take for that satellite to make one complete revolution around that planet? How does that compare with the length of time it takes for our planet's moon to make one complete revolution around Earth?

A TRIP TO OUTER SPACE: FACTS-TO-FIND

Part III—Challenge Questions

Provide well-written and detailed answers to at least one of the following sets of questions:

- How long would it take to travel from the planet Earth to the place you visited with our current technological limitations? How long would the entire voyage take if you traveled to your destination, stayed there for two weeks, then traveled back to Earth?
- What previous probes or other devices have been sent to the place you traveled to by scientists here on Earth? Are there any other probes or devices that are currently traveling toward the location you visited? Are there any probes or other devices that will be launched toward the place you visited in the near future?
- Can the place you traveled to ever be seen from Earth without the aid of a telescope or any other special viewing devices? Can it be seen from Earth with the help of binoculars or a telescope that you could buy in a store? Has it been seen only by specialized telescopes or space probes? Has it ever been seen by human beings? If the place you traveled to can be seen either without any special devices or with binoculars and/or a telescope that could be purchased in a store, when can it be seen and where in the sky would someone look to see it?

The Interdisciplinary Lesson Plan

Facilitating Investigation

A LESSON WELL LEARNED

Chapter 2 dealt with lesson planning by discussing the Culminating Task, through which students demonstrate what they know and can do. Lessons as discussed in this chapter—interdisciplinary lessons—refer to the experiences and investigations that prepare students to successfully undertake the culminating project. The seeds sown during the interdisciplinary lessons are harvested, so to speak, in the products or performances of the Culminating Task. John Barell (1997) reminds us that "units should organize lesson plans, not vice versa" (p. 31). That is why lesson planning is the last aspect of unit design to be addressed. The Interdisciplinary Lesson Plan specifically answers this question: What knowledge will students learn to successfully complete the Culminating Task? (See the blank Interdisciplinary Lesson Plan template in Appendix II: Planning Forms.)

APPROACHING CONTENT

The Lesson Perspective section of the Unit Planning Map introduces the following elements of the interdisciplinary lesson:

- Engaging the learner
- Exploring prior knowledge
- Exploring new ideas and concepts
- Elaborating on new learning

91

- Assessing student understanding
- Closure and reflection

Engaging the Learner

Engaging the learner is the first step in the process of instructional delivery. This hook intrigues learners to become emotionally involved enough to take the risks necessary to learn content. Motivation and emotion are key to this phase, because curiosity is piqued.

Exploring Prior Knowledge

This component helps students identify knowledge they already possess about the lesson concepts. The flip side of this process is that students also come to realize what they *don't* know about a topic. Teachers can target student misunderstandings and redirect them. Activities students take on in this phase help them retrieve information from their own schema that they then incorporate with the new ideas presented in the next phase.

Exploring New Ideas and Concepts

In this phase, teachers employ the kinds of strategies that facilitate active student learning (for example, inquiry, direct instruction, discovery, and demonstration) to introduce new content. Instructors collect data and make observations during this phase. Students interact with each other; use the Internet, artifacts, print resources, and topic experts; and conduct experiments and surveys to gain information and test hypotheses. Print- or lecture-exclusive presentation will not engage all learners at the same level. More dynamic methods of presentation and exploration of material are needed in order to create meaningful and lasting learning experiences. Suggestions for such experiences include:

- Field trips (actual and virtual)
- Storytelling
- Role playing
- Debating
- Lab experiments
- Graphic organizers
- Model making
- Storyboards

Elaborating on New Learning

Students process the information they gathered in the Exploring New Ideas phase to create a product or other evidence of understanding. Self-assessment and an observation checklist of group interaction are appropriate means of assessment during this phase. Students are asked to create meaning from the new ideas and clarify their understanding. Guided practice during this phase helps build and strengthen skills. Reflection and metacognition are an important part of this phase.

Assessing Student Understanding

Assessment in comprehensive interdisciplinary unit design and in lesson design is an ongoing opportunity for students to show what they know in various ways and in various situations. Rather than an ending or concluding phase of the lesson, assessing student understanding is a continuing, organic part of the lesson design.

Closure refers to the actions or statements by a teacher that are designed to bring the lesson to an appropriate conclusion. It is the act of reviewing and clarifying the key concepts of the lesson and tying those concepts together into a coherent whole.

Reflection is the metacognitive process that ensures practical application of the concepts learned by securing those concepts in the student's conceptual framework.

Both closure and reflection help the students to make sense out of what has just been taught. Together, they organize the learning in the students' minds and helps them form a coherent vision, eliminating confusion and/or frustration.

BEST-LAID PLANS

Planning and preparation are an essential part of good practice and a well-developed pedagogy, to be sure, but the proof is in the pudding. At the foundation of any successful plan are the teaching strategies a teacher chooses to use to bring that plan to life. Teachers need to select the strategies they will use for each lesson and for each group of students to whom it is taught. This requires that teachers have a growing number of strategies that they develop through continuous professional development and reflective self-assessment. A strategy that works with one group of students may not work with the next. Brain-compatible instructional strategies are among the many tools the successful teacher can put to use when presenting interdisciplinary instruction.

The following instructional strategies serve as the foundation of the lesson plan:

- Recognition of multiple intelligences and different student learning styles
- Use of cooperative learning that values and facilitates cooperative interdependence
- Inclusion of sensory-rich experiences
- Acknowledgment of the role of emotions in learning
- Maintenance of learning in a relevant context
- Planning of time for student reflection (metacognition)

AN ENVIRONMENT
THAT INSPIRES LEARNING

Life is a complex place, filled with challenge and choice. Research appears to indicate that the brain is adaptive and works best when making meaning out of complexity (Bruer, 1998). The classroom should reflect life's complexity without its more menacing features. It should be a complex and dynamic place. When well-designed lessons and units are presented in such an environment, their efficacy is intensified. Teachers can create and maintain a climate that inspires learning by making the environment:

- Visually exciting
- Safe for constructive risk taking and cooperative interaction
- Organized
- Rich in resources
- Filled with variety and choice

CHAPTER FIVE	Sample Unit

"Weathering the Storm"

Following is a sample interdisciplinary unit. This unit may be used as is or adjusted to fit the particular needs of your classroom.

WEATHERING THE STORM: CULMINATING TASK ORGANIZER

LESSON AT A GLANCE

CURRICULUM AREA(S): Language Arts, Social Studies, Science, Technology, Mathematics

GRADE LEVEL(S): 6–7

PROJECT DURATION: 4 weeks

RESOURCES/MATERIALS:
- Computers with Internet access to the National Weather Service's (NWS's) home page at http://www.nws.noaa.gov/
- University of Michigan Weather site (the Weather Underground) at http://cirrus.sprl.umich.edu/wxnet
- The NWS's Internet data source at http://iwin.nws.noaa.gov/iwin/main.html
- Word processor
- CD-ROM encyclopedia
- Rulers
- Various textbooks and/or reference books dealing with weather conditions
- Weather maps
- Old magazines (preferably ones that may contain pictures of any weather conditions)
- Index cards
- Graph paper
- Drawing paper and drawing supplies (crayons, markers, colored pencils, scissors, and so on)
- Thermometers and barometers
- Video of the movie *Twister*

TASK/PROJECT DESCRIPTION

In small groups of 2 or 3, students will utilize material researched and collected during unit lessons. Each group will create its own version of a magazine titled *Weathering the Storm*. The magazine will include at least 6 different types of weather, each weather type represented by at least one typed page of description and one illustration. The illustration can be from a magazine, newspaper, computer, or even hand drawn. The magazine must also include a line graph and a bar graph showing the high and low daily temperatures for one month. One page of the magazine should focus on one landform (located anywhere in the world) and discuss how weather has affected that area. The magazine is to begin with a colorful cover and close with a bibliography.

STANDARDS ADDRESSED

LANGUAGE ARTS	SCIENCE
1. Reading to build understanding 4. Spoken, written, and visual language for effective communication 6. Application of language structure and conventions to create, critique, and discuss 7. Research to generate ideas and questions, and pose problems 8. Technological and information resources to gather and synthesize information and to create and communicate knowledge 12. Spoken, written, and visual language to accomplish one's own purposes	A. Science as inquiry C. Life science **TECHNOLOGY** 3. Technology productivity tools 4. Technology communications tools

(Continued)

WEATHERING THE STORM: CULMINATING TASK ORGANIZER (Continued)

SOCIAL STUDIES	MATHEMATICS
3. People, places, and environments 8. Science, technology, and society	4. Measurement 5. Data analysis and probability

TASK/PROJECT OBJECTIVES

COMPREHENSION OF CONCEPTS	SKILL AND PROCESS DEVELOPMENT
At the end of this project, students will be able to . . . – Describe how the Sun affects weather, how clouds are formed, the differences in warm and cool air, the factors affecting weather, and the differences between a cold front and a warm front – Research weather conditions such as hurricanes, tornadoes, blizzards, and so on – Collect, record, and graph weather data for a month using a thermometer and/or a barometer – Create a magazine utilizing learned information about weather	At the end of this project, students will be able able to demonstrate . . . – Ability to share research with group members – Ability to find pertinent information – Teamwork – Ability to follow directions – Organizational skills – Ability to locate facts and information

PRODUCTS AND/OR PERFORMANCES

GROUP PRODUCTS	INDIVIDUAL PRODUCTS	EXTENSIONS
Completion of magazine – Line graphs and bar graphs – Discussion of weather's effect on land – Cover page – Bibliography A 5-minute team oral presentation of magazine	Magazine journal containing: – Notes in which knowledge of various types of weather conditions has been demonstrated – Graphing notes – Collection of either cutouts or original artwork illustrating specific weather conditions – Reflections on learning	– Share their magazines with their parents or with the rest of the school – Keep a log of the high and low temperatures for the day throughout the school year – Discuss the various types of weather conditions that occur while they are happening outside the school – Read fiction books about storms or other weather conditions

CRITERIA FOR TASK/PROJECT EVALUATION

GROUP PRODUCTS	INDIVIDUAL PRODUCTS	EXTENSIONS
– Knowledge level of various weather conditions – Quality of line and bar graphs (accuracy, readability, appearance) – Quality of weather-related artwork – Creative and technical writing qualities – Quality of presentation	– Knowledge and understanding of weather – Accuracy of line and bar graph notes – Quality and originality of artwork	– Students may be awarded extra points for working on extension activities.

WEATHERING THE STORM: WEATHER MAGAZINE ASSESSMENT RUBRIC							
Criteria Evaluated	1 Novice Beginning No, Not Yet	2 Basic Developing Yes, But	3 Proficient Accomplished Yes	4 Advanced Exemplary Yes Plus	RS*	DM	FS
Weather condition research	Fewer than 6 condition pages are included. Pages are of insufficient length and do not include detailed or relevant information about each specific weather condition.	All 6 weather conditions are included, but the pages may not all be the required length and creativity may not be consistent throughout.	All 6 weather conditions are included with detailed information about each condition.	More than 6 weather conditions are presented in a highly unique and creative manner. Each condition is articulated with complete accuracy and attention to detail.		5	
Pictures of weather conditions	Fewer than 4 weather pictures or drawings that accurately represent the particular weather condition are included.	At least 4 accurate weather pictures or drawings are included.	All 6 weather pictures or drawings are included. Each is a satisfactory representation of the particular weather condition.	More than 6 weather pictures/ drawings are stylishly presented in an innovative and creative manner, each with complete accuracy and attention to detail.		4	
Bar and line graphs	One or both of the graphs is missing data for more than one day.	One of the graphs is correct, but the other is missing data for one day.	Both graphs neatly and colorfully represent every day for one month.	Both graphs display sophisticated construction, are highly accurate, and are presented in a unique manner.		5	
Bibliography	Fewer than 5 sources are cited.	5 sources are cited, but none is set up in the proper format.	More than 5 sources are cited in the proper format.	More than 6 sources are cited, all in proper format.		3	
Cover	A cover is not included.	Cover is present, but it is neither neat nor colorful and/or shows a lack of effort.	Cover is neat and includes a title as well as team members' names.	Elegant cover is creative and colorful, with an attractive title and team members' names.		2	

(Continued)

WEATHERING THE STORM: WEATHER MAGAZINE ASSESSMENT RUBRIC (Continued)

Criteria Evaluated	1 Novice Beginning No, Not Yet	2 Basic Developing Yes, But	3 Proficient Accomplished Yes	4 Advanced Exemplary Yes Plus	RS*	DM	FS
Presentation	Not all group members contributed to the presentation. Relevant information was omitted.	All members of the group contributed to the presentation, but not everyone gave relevant information.	Each member of the group contributed to the presentation, offering relevant information.	Each member of the group played a vital role in the consistently high quality of the presentation.		2	
Weather's effect on landforms	Less than 1 typed page is submitted. The article lacks detailed and/or relevant information about weather's effect on this landform.	1 typed page is submitted, but relevant information about weather's effect on this landform has been omitted.	1 typed page is submitted with detailed and relevant information about weather's effect on this particular landform.	More than 1 typed page is submitted with highly accurate, detailed, and relevant information about weather's effect on this landform.		4	
				Total Grade			

*RS (raw score) refers to total of all initial points achieved. Multiply raw score by difficulty multiplier (DM) for final score (FS).

WEATHERING THE STORM: UNIT PLANNING MAP

UNIT AT A GLANCE	LESSON 1: Homemade Tornado (Tornado in a Bottle)	LESSON 1 PERSPECTIVE

TOPIC: Weather
CURRICULUM AREA(S): Language Arts, Social Studies, Science, Technology, Mathematics
GRADE LEVEL(S): 6
PROJECT DURATION: 4 weeks
UNIT OBJECTIVES:
At the end of the unit, students will be able to . . .
  – Increase their understanding of how different types of weather conditions actually develop
	OBJECTIVES: Students will be able to . . .
	  – Explain the dynamics of a tornado and its formation
	ACTIVITIES:
	Student will . . .
	  – Create "bottle" tornadoes
		ENGAGING THE LEARNER: Students will watch video clip from the movie *Twister*.
		EXPLORING PRIOR KNOWLEDGE: Principles of gravity.
		EXPLORING NEW IDEAS/CONCEPTS: Tornado formation and perpetuation.
		ELABORATING ON NEW LEARNING: Students will explain tornado formation.
		ASSESSING STUDENT UNDERSTANDING: Teacher observations and class discussions.
		CLOSURE/REFLECTION: Students will share tornado models.

WEATHERING THE STORM: UNIT PLANNING MAP

UNIT AT A GLANCE	LESSON 2: Cloudscape Model	LESSON 2 PERSPECTIVE
TECHNOLOGY: Teacher and students will use various technological tools to enhance student learning. ASSESSMENT: – Student journals will be used for group discussion as well as evaluation. – 5-minute oral presentation evaluated by student-designed rubric.	OBJECTIVES: Students will be able to . . . – Describe differences among the various cloud types – Predict weather possibilities of each cloud type ACTIVITIES: Students will work in pairs to . . . – Classify various cloud types – Create "cloudscape" models	ENGAGING THE LEARNER: Students will view the *Fresh Science* DVD and examine books illustrating different cloud classifications. EXPLORING PRIOR KNOWLEDGE: Discuss origin of rain. EXPLORING NEW IDEAS/CONCEPTS: Different cloud types produce different weather conditions. ELABORATING ON NEW LEARNING: Students share their learning with others. ASSESSING STUDENT UNDERSTANDING: Teacher interviews individual students about different cloud types while they work on cloudscape project. CLOSURE/REFLECTION: Journal reflections on various cloud types.
	LESSON 3: Internet Forecasting	LESSON 3 PERSPECTIVE
	OBJECTIVES: Students will be able to . . . – Demonstrate Internet capabilities by locating, retrieving, graphing, and interpreting data ACTIVITIES: Students will . . . – Use the Internet to locate weather data resources – Compare temperature differences of select cities	ENGAGING THE LEARNER: Familiarize students with researching on the Internet. EXPLORING PRIOR KNOWLEDGE: Provide weather Web sites for students to explore and gather data. EXPLORING NEW IDEAS/CONCEPTS: Students will compare regional weather variations. ELABORATING ON NEW LEARNING: Using a Web site that enables users to graph temperature variations among different regions, students will graph data and write explanations. ASSESSING STUDENT UNDERSTANDING: Teacher observes students at computers and then reviews and assesses required written work. CLOSURE/REFLECTION: Review process of finding weather information on the Internet.

(Continued)

WEATHERING THE STORM: UNIT PLANNING MAP (Continued)

	LESSON 4: Hurricanes	LESSON 4 PERSPECTIVE
	OBJECTIVES: Students will be able to . . . – Define a hurricane – Explain hurricane formation and track where they form ACTIVITIES: Students will . . . – Research conditions resulting in hurricane formation as well as measures that can be taken for hurricane preparation	ENGAGING THE LEARNER: Students will take a "virtual" field trip. EXPLORING PRIOR KNOWLEDGE: Students will discuss personal experiences with hurricanes. EXPLORING NEW IDEAS/CONCEPTS: Students will watch a hurricane in motion via the Internet. ELABORATING ON NEW LEARNING: Students will share knowledge with the class. ASSESSING STUDENT UNDERSTANDING: Does "hurricane in a bottle" work? CLOSURE/REFLECTION: Students use new vocabulary words in a paragraph.

WEATHERING THE STORM: INTERDISCIPLINARY LESSON PLAN: INTERNET FORECASTING

LESSON AT A GLANCE

CURRICULUM AREA(S): Language Arts, Science, Mathematics, Technology
GRADE LEVEL(S): 6
LESSON DURATION: 1–2 days
PREPARATION, RESOURCES, AND MATERIALS: Computers with Internet access, paper, pencils

INSTRUCTIONAL OBJECTIVES	ONGOING ASSESSMENT
At the end of the lesson, students will be able to demonstrate Internet skills by locating, retrieving, and interpreting data.	• Observe students as they work at computers. • Review and assess written work.

STANDARDS ADDRESSED

LANGUAGE ARTS	SCIENCE
4. Spoken, written, and visual language for effective communication 8. Technological and information resources to gather and synthesize information and to create and communicate knowledge	A. Scientific inquiry E. Science and technology

MATHEMATICS	TECHNOLOGY
5. Data analysis and probability 9. Connections	1. Basic operations and concepts 5. Technology research tools

WEATHERING THE STORM: INTERDISCIPLINARY LESSON PLAN: INTERNET FORECASTING

STEPS/PROCEDURES

1. ENGAGING THE LEARNER	2. EXPLORING PRIOR KNOWLEDGE
Guide discussion in which students are asked to list sources to learn about tomorrow's weather (for example, television and newspaper). Introduce Internet as a source.	Provide students with several Internet sites and ask them to gather and record specified data from each site (www.ncdc.noaa.gov).
3. EXPLORING NEW IDEAS	**4. ELABORATING ON NEW LEARNING**
Have students explore various Web sites to compare regional weather variations.	Once students have accomplished data gathering, provide instructions to graph temperature difference between different cities. (They can pick two cities of their choice and create a graph of the temperature differences.)
5. ASSESSING STUDENT UNDERSTANDING	**6. CLOSURE AND REFLECTION**
Observe students at computers and have each student write a paragraph describing his or her graph and explain his or her thoughts as to why there is a temperature discrepancy.	Review as a class the process of finding weather-related information on the Internet. Have students discuss which two cities they chose to graph temperature variations, why they chose them, and what they learned from the activity.
7. METHODS FOR DIFFERENTIATION OF INSTRUCTION	**8. LESSON FOLLOW-UP AND TEACHER REFLECTION**
Visual learners: Computers as information source Kinesthetic learners: Use of computer keyboard to help process information Auditory learners: Verbal instructions and support	Students will follow an aberrant weather situation somewhere in the world and report on its progress.

Appendix I

Content Area Standards

ONLINE STATE CONTENT STANDARDS

Alabama	http://alex.state.al.us/browseStand.php
Alaska	http://www.eed.state.ak.us/contentStandards/
Arizona	http://www.ade.state.az.us/sbtl/sdi/
Arkansas	http://www.arkansased.org/teachers/ frameworks2.html
California	http://www.cde.ca.gov/be/st/ss/
Colorado	http://www.cde.state.co.us/cdeassess/ documents/OLR/k12_standards.html
Connecticut	http://www.state.ct.us/sde/DTL/ curriculum/index.htm
Delaware	http://www.doe.k12.de.us/programs/pcs/
District of Columbia	http://www.k12.dc.us/dcps/Standards/ standardsHome.htm
Florida	http://www.firn.edu/doe/menu/sss.htm
Georgia	http://www.georgiastandards.org/
Hawaii	http://www.hcps.k12.hi.us/
Idaho	http://www.boardofed.idaho.gov/saa/ standards.asp
Illinois	http://www.isbe.state.il.us/ils/Default.htm
Indiana	http://ideanet.doe.state.in.us/standards/ welcome.html
Kansas	http://www.ksde.org/
Maryland	http://mdk12.org/mspp/vsc/
Massachusetts	http://www.doe.mass.edu/frameworks/ current.html

Michigan	http://www.michigan.gov/mde/
Minnesota	http://www.education.state.mn.us/mde/Academic_Excellence/Academic_Standards/index.html
Mississippi	http://www.mde.k12.ms.us/Curriculum/index_1.htm
Missouri	http://dese.mo.gov/standards/
Montana	http://www.opi.state.mt.us/Accred/cstandards.html
Nebraska	http://www.nde.state.ne.us/ndestandards/AcadStand.html
Nevada	http://www.doe.nv.gov/standards.html
New Hampshire	http://www.ed.state.nh.us/education/doe/organization/curriculum/CurriculumFrameworks/CurriculumFrameworks.htm
New Jersey	http://www.state.nj.us/njded/aps/cccs/
New Mexico	http://www.ped.state.nm.us/standards/index.html
North Carolina	http://www.ncpublicschools.org/curriculum/ncscos
North Dakota	http://www.dpi.state.nd.us/standard/index.shtm
Ohio	http://www.ode.state.oh.us/
Oklahoma	http://www.sde.state.ok.us/publ/pass.html
Oregon	http://www.ode.state.or.us/
Pennsylvania	http://www.pde.state.pa.us/
Rhode Island	http://www.ridoe.net/standards/
South Carolina	http://ed.sc.gov/agency/offices/cso/
South Dakota	http://doe.sd.gov/contentstandards/
Tennessee	http://www.state.tn.us/education/ci/standards/
Texas	http://www.tea.state.tx.us/teks/
Utah	http://www.schools.utah.gov/curr/core/
Vermont	http://education.vermont.gov/new/html/pubs/framework.html
Virginia	http://www.pen.k12.va.us/go/Sols/home.shtml
Washington	http://www.k12.wa.us/CurriculumInstruct/default.aspx
West Virginia	http://wvde.state.wv.us/policies/csos.html
Wisconsin	http://dpi.state.wi.us/standards/
Wyoming	http://www.k12.wy.us/SA/standards.asp

PROFESSIONAL ORGANIZATIONS' WEB SITES RELATED TO STANDARDS

Center for Education Reform	http://edreform.com/standard.htm
Council of Chief State School Officers	http://www.ccsso.org/projects/browse_by_topic/index.cfm

STANDARDS AND THE NATURE OF SCHOOL MATHEMATICS: NATIONAL COUNCIL OF TEACHERS OF MATHEMATICS

Past approaches to teaching mathematics tended to fragment the discipline into separate and discrete subdivisions that lacked any meaningful connection. Through its first set of standards documents, however, the National Council of Teachers of Mathematics (NCTM) provided leadership, focus, and coherence to the efforts to improve mathematics education (see Figure A.1). Since its first publication in 1989, the NCTM's *Curriculum and Evaluation Standards* has greatly influenced the way we think about teaching mathematics. In its introduction, the NCTM offered three reasons for professional organizations to formally adopt standards: to ensure quality, to indicate goals, and to promote change.

The original NCTM standards documents made the following clear:

- A range of pedagogical strategies is necessary to support students' mathematics learning.
- Students learn to reason and communicate mathematically only if they have the opportunity to do so.
- Individual, small-group, and whole-class instruction are all necessary components of a well-orchestrated mathematics learning environment.

The documents also made it clear that assessment at all levels—assessment of individual students, of the instructional environment, and of all aspects of the instructional system—is an integral part of the teaching-learning process and not merely a summative "add on" at a unit's end.

An Overview of the New Principles and Standards

The goals for the current *Principles and Standards for School Mathematics* (1) build upon the foundations of the original NCTM standards documents, (2) consolidate the classroom aspects of those three documents, and (3) organize the new document into four grade band sections, thereby allowing more detail and specificity for the grades.

The current *Principles and Standards* strengthens and furthers the message of the original standards documents by including the following items:

- A common set of ten standards (see Figure A.2) that articulate the growth of mathematical knowledge across the grades, rather than a different set and number for each grade band
- Four grade bands (PreK–2, 3–5, 6–8, 9–12) instead of three, allowing more focus on, and detail for, the elementary and middle grades
- Recommendations for the mathematical learning of preschool children

Figure A.1 How Did We Get Here?

A Nation at Risk warns we are being over-come by a "rising tide of mediocrity"

1983

American Association for the Advancement of Science initiates Science for All Americans (Project 2061) NCTM Collaborates with NRC (National Research Council)

Mid-1980s

President Bush convenes governors for an educational summit resulting in Goals 2000

Late 1980s

NCTM Mathematics Standards

1989

National Science Education Standards (NSES)

1994

Third International Mathematics and Science Study (TIMSS)

1996–98

Efforts made to create Standards for the Language Arts, the Social Studies, and Technology

Late 1990s

- A new standard on representation that outlines the processes and outcomes of acquiring and demonstrating mathematical concepts mentally, symbolically, and graphically, and by using physical materials
- The addition of principles that outline particular characteristics of high-quality mathematics education that can be used as a guide for decision making
- Significantly more citations from research to support the assertions made
- An electronic edition (E-Standards) in addition to the printed document

Figure A.2   NCTM Principles and Standards for School Mathematics

---

STANDARD 1: NUMBERS AND OPERATIONS

Instructional programs from pre-kindergarten through Grade 12 should enable all students to
- Understand numbers, ways of representing numbers, relationships among numbers, and number systems
- Understand meanings of operations and how they relate to one another, and
- Compute fluently and make reasonable estimates

STANDARD 2: ALGEBRA

Instructional programs from pre-kindergarten through Grade 12 should enable all students to
- Understand patterns, relations, and functions
- Represent and analyze mathematical situations and structures using algebraic symbols
- Use mathematical models to represent and understand quantitative relationships, and
- Analyze change in various contexts

STANDARD 3: GEOMETRY

Instructional programs from pre-kindergarten through Grade 12 should enable all students to
- Analyze characteristics and properties of two- and three-dimensional geometric shapes and develop mathematical arguments about geometric relationships
- Specify locations and describe spatial relationships using coordinate geometry and other representational systems
- Apply transformations and use symmetry to analyze mathematical situations, and
- Use visualization, spatial reasoning, and geometric modeling to solve problems

STANDARD 4: MEASUREMENT

Instructional programs from pre-kindergarten through Grade 12 should enable all students to
- Understand measurable attributes of objects and the units, systems, and processes of measurement; and
- Apply appropriate techniques, tools, and formulas to determine measurements

STANDARD 5: DATA ANALYSIS AND PROBABILITY

Instructional programs from pre-kindergarten through Grade 12 should enable all students to
- Formulate questions that can be addressed with data and collect, organize, and display relevant data to answer them
- Select and use appropriate statistical methods to analyze data
- Develop and evaluate inferences and predictions that are based on data, and
- Understand and apply basic concepts of probability

(Continued)

Figure A.2 (Continued)

STANDARD 6: PROBLEM SOLVING

Instructional programs from pre-kindergarten through Grade 12 should enable all students to
- Build new mathematical knowledge through problem solving
- Solve problems that arise in mathematics and in other contexts
- Apply and adapt a variety of appropriate strategies to solve problems, and
- Monitor and reflect on the process of mathematical problem solving

STANDARD 7: REASONING AND PROOF

Instructional programs from pre-kindergarten through Grade 12 should enable all students to
- Recognize reasoning and proof as fundamental aspects of mathematics
- Make and investigate mathematical conjectures
- Develop and evaluate mathematical arguments and proofs, and
- Select and use various types of reasoning and methods of proof

STANDARD 8: COMMUNICATION

Instructional programs from pre-kindergarten through Grade 12 should enable all students to
- Organize and consolidate their mathematical thinking through communication
- Communicate their mathematical thinking coherently and clearly to peers, teachers, and others
- Analyze and evaluate the mathematical thinking and strategies of others, and
- Use the language of mathematics to express mathematical ideas precisely

STANDARD 9: CONNECTIONS

Instructional programs from pre-kindergarten through Grade 12 should enable all students to
- Recognize and use connections among mathematical ideas
- Understand how mathematical ideas interconnect and build on one another to produce a coherent whole, and
- Recognize and apply mathematics in contexts outside of mathematics

STANDARD 10: REPRESENTATION

Instructional programs from pre-kindergarten through Grade 12 should enable all students to
- Create and use representations to organize, record, and communicate mathematical ideas
- Select, apply, and translate among mathematical representations to solve problems, and
- Use representations to model and interpret physical, social, and mathematical phenomena

---

SOURCE: Principles and standards have been adapted from *Principles and Standards for School Mathematics.* © 2000–2004 by the National Council of Teachers of Mathematics, Inc.

Mathematics Instructional Program Principles

In addition to the ten standards, the following six principles describe basic convictions about high-quality mathematics instructional programs and provide guidance for making decisions that influence students' learning opportunities. The principles apply at many levels of the educational system and thus encourage and support systemic change. The principles also express the perspectives and assumptions that underlie the ten standards. The principles are as follows:

1. *Equity*

Excellence in mathematics education requires equity—high expectations and strong support for all students. (Mathematics instructional programs should promote the learning of mathematics by all students.)

2. *Curriculum*

A curriculum is more than a collection of activities: it must be coherent, focused on important mathematics, and well articulated across the grades. (Mathematics instructional programs should emphasize important and meaningful mathematics through curricula that are coherent and comprehensive.)

3. *Teaching*

Effective mathematics teaching requires understanding of what students know and need to learn and then challenging them and supporting them to learn it well. (Mathematics instructional programs depend on competent and caring teachers who teach all students to understand and use mathematics.)

4. *Learning*

Students must learn mathematics with understanding, actively building new knowledge from experience and prior knowledge. (Mathematics instructional programs should enable all students to understand and use mathematics.)

5. *Assessment*

Assessment should support the learning of important mathematics and furnish useful information to both teachers and students. (Mathematics instructional programs should include assessment to monitor, enhance, and evaluate the mathematics learning of all students and to inform teaching.)

6. *Technology*

Technology is essential in teaching and learning mathematics; it influences the mathematics that is taught and enhances students' learning. (Mathematics instructional programs should use technology to help all students understand mathematics and should prepare them to use mathematics in an increasingly technological world.)

An electronic version of *Principles and Standards* is available online at http://standards.nctm.org/.

NCTM's *Principles and Standards* sets the following goals for the teaching and learning of mathematics:

- Learning mathematics with understanding and acquiring the skills and knowledge needed to solve mathematical problems
- Having an in-depth knowledge of the traditional basics of mathematics as well as the new basics, such as data analysis and statistics, needed for the technological world in which we live
- Developing reasoning skills that will engender flexible and resourceful problem solving

School mathematics education bears increasing responsibilities in a data-rich era. Mathematics instructional programs should provide individuals access to mathematical ideas and should promote students' abilities to reason analytically. In a society saturated with quantitative information ranging from global climate change data to political polls and consumer reports, such skills will help students to understand, make informed decisions about, and affect their world. School mathematics education should contribute to public awareness of the discipline's contributions to society. It should also help enable people to determine the social and economic consequences of their own decisions as well as those made by elected representatives on their behalf.

THE NATIONAL
SCIENCE EDUCATION STANDARDS

The *National Science Education Standards* (NSES) (National Academy of Sciences, 1996) presents a vision of a scientifically literate populace. These standards (see Figure A.3) outline what students need to know, understand, and be able to do to be scientifically literate at different grade levels. They describe an educational system in which all students demonstrate high levels of performance, teachers are empowered to make the decisions essential for effective learning, interlocking communities of teachers and students are focused on learning science, and supportive educational programs and systems nurture achievement.

The standards rest on the premise that *science is an active process.* "Learning" science is something those students "do," not something that is "done" to them. "Hands-on" activities, while essential, are not enough. Students must have "minds-on" experiences as well. To do this, the standards call for more than "science as process," in which students learn such skills as observing, inferring, and experimenting. What these standards call for is an emphasis on inquiry itself as being central to science learning. When engaging in inquiry, students describe objects and events, ask questions, construct explanations, test those explanations against current scientific knowledge, and communicate their ideas to others. They identify their assumptions, use critical and logical thinking, and consider alternative explanations. In this manner, students actively develop their own understanding of science by combining scientific knowledge with reasoning and thinking skills.

INTERNATIONAL SOCIETY
FOR TECHNOLOGY IN EDUCATION

To adequately prepare our children for adult citizenship in the Information Age, computer-related technology must become a tool that both students and teachers use routinely. However, information technology alone cannot solve all of education's problems. To achieve meaningful learning, the classroom environment must provide ample opportunities for communication, decision making, and genuine problem solving to occúr. (See Figure A.4.) Like traditional

(Text continued on page 115)

Figure A.3   Science Standards

GRADES K–4

CONTENT STANDARD A: SCIENCE AS INQUIRY

A1. Abilities necessary to do scientific inquiry:
  - Ask a question about objects, organisms, and events in the environment.
  - Plan and conduct a simple investigation.
  - Employ simple equipment and tools to gather data and extend the senses.
  - Use data to construct a reasonable explanation.
  - Communicate investigations and explanations.

A2. Understandings about scientific inquiry:
  - Scientific investigations involve asking and answering a question and comparing the answer with what scientists already know about the world.
  - Scientists use different kinds of investigations depending on the questions they are trying to answer.
  - Simple instruments provide more information than scientists obtain using only their senses.
  - Scientists develop explanations using observations (evidence) and what they already know about the world (scientific knowledge).
  - Scientists make the results of their investigations public; they describe the investigations in ways that enable others to repeat the investigations.
  - Scientists review and ask questions about the results of other scientists' work.

CONTENT STANDARD B: PHYSICAL SCIENCE

B1. Properties of objects and materials
B2. Position and motion of objects
B3. Light, heat, electricity, and magnetism

CONTENT STANDARD C: LIFE SCIENCE

C1. The characteristics of organisms
C2. Life cycles of organisms
C3. Organisms and environments

CONTENT STANDARD D: EARTH AND SPACE SCIENCE

D1. Properties of Earth materials
D2. Objects in the sky
D3. Changes in earth and sky

CONTENT STANDARD E: SCIENCE AND TECHNOLOGY

E1. Abilities of technological design
E2. Understanding about science and technology
E3. Abilities to distinguish between natural objects and objects made by humans

CONTENT STANDARD F: SCIENCE IN PERSONAL AND SOCIAL PERSPECTIVES

F1. Personal health
F2. Characteristics and changes in populations
F3. Types of resources
F4. Changes in environments
F5. Science and technology in local challenges

CONTENT STANDARD G: HISTORY AND NATURE OF SCIENCE

G1. Science as a human endeavor:
  - Science and technology have been practiced by people for a long time.
  - Men and women have made a variety of contributions throughout the history of science and technology.
  - Science will never be finished.
  - Many people choose science as a career.

(Continued)

Figure A.3 (Continued)

GRADES 5–8

CONTENT STANDARD A: SCIENCE AS INQUIRY

A1. Abilities necessary to do scientific inquiry:
- Identify questions that can be answered through scientific investigations.
- Design and conduct a scientific investigation.
- Use appropriate tools and techniques to gather, analyze, and interpret data.
- Develop descriptions, explanations, predictions, and models using evidence and explanations.
- Think critically and logically to make the relationships between evidence and explanations.
- Recognize and analyze alternative explanations and predictions.
- Communicate scientific procedures and explanations.
- Use mathematics in all aspects of scientific inquiry.

A2. Understandings about scientific inquiry:
- Different kinds of questions suggest different kinds of scientific investigations.
- Current scientific knowledge and understanding guide scientific investigations.
- Mathematics is important in all aspects of scientific inquiry.
- Technology used to gather data enhances accuracy and allows scientists to analyze and quantify results of investigations.
- Scientific explanations emphasize evidence, have logically consistent arguments, and use scientific principles, models, and theories.
- Science advances through legitimate skepticism.
- Scientific investigations sometimes result in new ideas and phenomena.

CONTENT STANDARD B: PHYSICAL SCIENCE

B1. Properties and changes of properties in matter
B2. Motions and forces
B3. Transfer of energy

CONTENT STANDARD C: LIFE SCIENCE

C1. Structure and function in living systems
C2. Reproduction and heredity
C3. Regulation and behavior
C4. Populations and ecosystems
C5. Diversity and adaptations of organisms

CONTENT STANDARD D: EARTH AND SPACE SCIENCE

D1. Structure of the earth system
D2. Earth's history
D3. Earth in the solar system

CONTENT STANDARD E: SCIENCE AND TECHNOLOGY

E1. Abilities of technological design:
- Identify appropriate problems for technological design.
- Design a solution or product.
- Implement a proposed design.
- Evaluate completed technological designs or products.
- Communicate the process of technological design.

E2. Understandings about science and technology:
- Scientific inquiry and technological design have similarities and differences.
- Many different people in different cultures have made and continue to make contributions to science and technology.
- Science and technology are reciprocal.
- Perfectly designed solutions do not exist.
- Technological designs have constraints.
- Technological solutions have intended benefits and unintended consequences.

CONTENT STANDARD F: SCIENCE IN PERSONAL AND SOCIAL PERSPECTIVES

F1. Personal health
F2. Populations, resources, and environments
F3. Natural hazards
F4. Risks and benefits
F5. Science and technology in society

CONTENT STANDARD G: HISTORY AND NATURE OF SCIENCE

G1. Science as a human endeavor:
  • Women and men of various social and ethnic backgrounds engage in the activities of science, engineering, and related fields.
  • Science requires different abilities.

G2. Nature of science:
  • Scientists formulate and test their explanations of nature using observation, experiments, and theoretical and mathematical models.
  • It is normal for scientists to differ with one another about the interpretation of the evidence or theory being considered.
  • It is part of scientific inquiry to evaluate ideas proposed by other scientists.

G3. History of science:
  • Many individuals have contributed to the traditions of science.
  • In historical perspective, science has been practiced by different individuals in different cultures.
  • Tracing the history of science can show how difficult it was for scientific innovators to break through the accepted ideas of their time to reach the conclusions that we currently take for granted.

GRADES 9–12
CONTENT STANDARD A: SCIENCE AS INQUIRY

A1. Abilities necessary to do scientific inquiry:
  • Identify questions and concepts that guide scientific investigations.
  • Design and conduct scientific investigations.
  • Use technology and mathematics to improve investigations and communications.
  • Formulate and revise scientific explanations and models using logic and evidence.
  • Recognize and analyze alternative explanations and models.
  • Communicate and defend a scientific argument.

A2. Understandings about scientific inquiry:
  • Scientists usually inquire about how physical, living, or designed systems function.
  • Scientists conduct investigations for a wide variety of reasons.
  • Scientists rely on technology to enhance the gathering and manipulation of data.
  • Mathematics is essential in scientific inquiry.
  • Scientific explanations must adhere to criteria. For example, a proposed explanation must be logically consistent; it must abide by the rules of evidence; it must be open to questions and possible modification; and it must be based on historical and current scientific knowledge.
  • Results of scientific inquiry emerge from different types of investigations and public communication among scientists.

CONTENT STANDARD B: PHYSICAL SCIENCE

B1. Structure of atoms
B2. Structure and properties of matter
B3. Chemical reactions
B4. Motions and forces
B5. Conservation of energy and increase in disorder
B6. Interactions of energy and matter

CONTENT STANDARD C: LIFE SCIENCE

C1. The cell
C2. Molecular basis of heredity

Figure A.3 (Continued)

C3. Biological evolution
C4. Interdependence of organisms
C5. Matter, energy, and organization in living systems
C6. Behavior of organisms

CONTENT STANDARD D: EARTH AND SPACE SCIENCE

D1. Energy in the earth system
D2. Geochemical cycles
D3. Origin and evolution of the earth system
D4. Origin and evolution of the universe

CONTENT STANDARD E: SCIENCE AND TECHNOLOGY

E1. Abilities of technological design:
   • Identify a problem or design an opportunity.
   • Propose designs and choose between alternative solutions.
   • Implement a proposed solution.
   • Evaluate the solution and its consequences.
   • Communicate the problem, process, and solution.

E2. Understandings about science and technology:
   • Scientists in different disciplines ask different questions, use different methods of investigation, and accept different types of evidence to support their explanations.
   • Science often advances with the introduction of new technologies.
   • Creativity, imagination, and a good knowledge base are all required in the work of science and engineering.
   • Science and technology are pursued for different purposes.
   • Technological knowledge is often not made public because of patents and the financial potential of the idea or invention. Scientific knowledge is made public.

CONTENT STANDARD F: SCIENCE IN PERSONAL AND SOCIAL PERSPECTIVES

F1. Personal and community health
F2. Population growth
F3. Natural resources
F4. Environmental quality
F5. Natural and human-induced hazards
F6. Science and technology in local, national, and global challenges

CONTENT STANDARD G: HISTORY AND NATURE OF SCIENCE

G1. Science as a human endeavor:
   • Individuals and teams have contributed and will continue to contribute to the scientific enterprise.
   • Scientists have ethical traditions.
   • Scientists are influenced by societal, cultural, and personal beliefs and ways of viewing the world.

G2. Nature of scientific knowledge:
   • Science distinguishes itself from other ways of knowing and from other bodies of knowledge.
   • Scientific explanations must meet certain criteria.
   • Because all scientific ideas depend on experimental and observational confirmation, all scientific knowledge is, in principle, subject to change as new evidence becomes available.

G3. Historical perspectives:
   • In history, diverse cultures have contributed scientific knowledge and technologic inventions.
   • Usually, changes in science occur as small modifications in extant knowledge.
   • Occasionally, there are advances in science and technology that have important and long-lasting effects on science and society.
   • The historical perspective of scientific explanations demonstrates how scientific knowledge changes by evolving over time, almost always building on earlier knowledge.

SOURCE: Adapted from *National Science Education Standards.* © 1997 by the National Academy of Sciences. Courtesy of the National Academy Press, Washington, D.C.

Figure A.4   Technology Foundation Standards for Students

1. **BASIC OPERATIONS AND CONCEPTS**
   - Students demonstrate a sound understanding of the nature and operation of technology systems.
   - Students are proficient in the use of technology.

2. **SOCIAL, ETHICAL, AND HUMAN ISSUES**
   - Students understand the ethical, cultural, and societal issues related to technology.
   - Students practice responsible use of technology systems, information, and software.
   - Students develop positive attitudes toward technology uses that support lifelong learning, collaboration, personal pursuits, and productivity.

3. **TECHNOLOGY PRODUCTIVITY TOOLS**
   - Students use technology tools to enhance learning, increase productivity, and promote creativity.
   - Students use productivity tools to collaborate in constructing technology-enhanced models, prepare publications, and produce other creative works.

4. **TECHNOLOGY COMMUNICATIONS TOOLS**
   - Students use telecommunications to collaborate, publish, and interact with peers, experts, and other audiences.
   - Students use a variety of media and formats to communicate information and ideas effectively to multiple audiences.

5. **TECHNOLOGY RESEARCH TOOLS**
   - Students use technology to locate, evaluate, and collect information from a variety of sources.
   - Students use technology tools to process data and report results.
   - Students evaluate and select new information resources and technological innovations based on the appropriateness for specific tasks.

6. **TECHNOLOGY PROBLEM-SOLVING AND DECISION-MAKING TOOLS**
   - Students use technology resources for solving problems and making informed decisions.
   - Students employ technology in the development of strategies for solving problems in the real world.

technologies (books, pencils and paper, overhead projectors, chalk boards, slide and film projectors, and so on), computers and Internet resources provide only a means to achieving an end. What matters ultimately is the experience that learners have and what they make of that experience.

These technology goals align with the problem-based learning (PBL) philosophy, which is student centered and inquiry based. Technology provides students with one of the most important tools for solving challenges and/or problem tasks. Research is the basis of problem solving, and technology levels the research playing field to enable even young children to locate the information they need.

The world of the not-too-distant future will be firmly planted on a technological foundation. For today's students to develop into tomorrow's productive citizens, they will need to use technology the way their predecessors used pencil and paper—as the very building blocks of learning.

LANGUAGE ARTS, THE NCTE/IRA, AND PROBLEM-BASED LEARNING

The National Council of Teachers of English (NCTE) and the International Reading Association (IRA) assert that all students must have the opportunities and resources to develop the language skills that will enable them to pursue their life's goals and to participate fully as informed, productive members of society. The NCTE/IRA standards (see Figure A.5) assume that literacy growth begins before children enter school: literacy skills begin developing as children experience and experiment with reading, writing, and associating spoken words with their graphic representations. Recognizing this fact, these standards encourage the development of curriculum and instruction that make productive use of the emerging literacy abilities that children bring to school.

Furthermore, the standards are not designed to be prescriptions for particular curricula or instruction. In fact, they provide ample room for the innovation and creativity essential to teaching and learning. They are very much learner centered in that they focus on the ways in which students actively participate in their learning, acquire knowledge, shape experience, and respond to their own particular needs and goals through language arts.

It should be emphasized that these standards, though presented in a list, are not distinct and separable. Rather, they are interrelated and should be considered as a whole. Although the list format might suggest that knowledge and understanding can be sliced into tidy and distinct categories, literacy learning (like any other area of human learning) is far more complicated than that. Complex relationships exist among the standards. Further, the standards cannot and should not be translated into isolated components of instruction. On the contrary: virtually any instructional activity will likely address multiple standards simultaneously.

STANDARDS FOR THE SOCIAL STUDIES

According to the National Council for the Social Studies (NCSS):

> Social Studies is the integrated study of the social sciences and humanities to promote civic competence. Within the school program, social studies provides coordinated, systematic study drawing upon such disciplines as anthropology, archaeology, economics, geography, history, law, philosophy, political science, psychology, religion, and sociology, as well as appropriate content from the humanities, mathematics, and natural sciences. The primary purpose of social studies is to help young people develop the ability to make informed and reasoned decisions for the public good as citizens of a culturally diverse, democratic society in an interdependent world.

The standards do not represent a set of mandated outcomes or establish a national curriculum for the social studies. Rather, they should be used as

Figure A.5   NCTE/IRA Standards for the English Language Arts

1. Students read a wide range of print and nonprint texts to build an understanding of texts, of themselves, and of the cultures of the United States and the world; to acquire new information; to respond to the needs and demands of society and the workplace; and for personal fulfillment. Among these texts are fiction and nonfiction, classic and contemporary works.

2. Students read a wide range of literature from many periods in many genres to build an understanding of the many dimensions (for example, philosophical, ethical, and aesthetic) of human experience.

3. Students apply a wide range of strategies to comprehend, interpret, evaluate, and appreciate texts. They draw on their prior experience, their interactions with other readers and writers, their knowledge of word meaning and of other texts, their word identification strategies, and their understanding of textual features (for example, sound-letter correspondence, sentence structure, context, and graphics).

4. Students adjust their use of spoken, written, and visual language (for example, conventions, style, and vocabulary) to communicate effectively with a variety of audiences and for different purposes.

5. Students employ a wide range of strategies as they write and use different writing process elements appropriately to communicate with different audiences for a variety of purposes.

6. Students apply knowledge of language structure, language conventions (for example, spelling and punctuation), media techniques, figurative language, and genre to create, critique, and discuss print and nonprint texts.

7. Students conduct research on issues and interests by generating ideas and questions, and by posing problems. They gather, evaluate, and synthesize data from a variety of sources (for example, print and nonprint texts, artifacts, and people) to communicate their discoveries in ways that suit their purpose and audience.

8. Students use a variety of technological and information resources (for example, libraries, databases, computer networks, and video) to gather and synthesize information and to create and communicate knowledge.

9. Students develop an understanding of and respect for diversity in language use, patterns, and dialects across cultures, ethnic groups, geographic regions, and social roles.

10. Students whose first language is not English make use of their first language to develop competency in the English language arts and to develop understanding of content across the curriculum.

11. Students participate as knowledgeable, reflective, creative, and critical members of a variety of literacy communities.

12. Students use spoken, written, and visual language to accomplish their own purposes (for example, for learning, enjoyment, persuasion, and the exchange of information).

SOURCE: Adapted from *Standards for the English Language Arts* (1998–2006), International Reading Association and the National Council of Teachers of English. Copyright 1996 by the International Reading Association and the National Council of Teachers of English. Reprinted with permission (http://www.ncte.org/about/over/standards/110846.htm).

guides and criteria to establish integrated state, district, school, department, and classroom curriculum plans to guide instruction, learning, and assessment. Except for clustering the standards into early grades, middle grades, and high school grades, there is no specified sequence that must be followed or subject matter content that must be taught. Decisions such as scope, specific content, and sequence are in the hands of those who are seeking to improve their social studies curricula to increase the quality of their students' social studies knowledge and skills. These state and local decisions will augment and enhance the framework these national standards provide.

Standards Developed by the National Council for the Social Studies

The *Curriculum Standards for Social Studies* present a set of ten thematically based curriculum standards, or statements of what should occur programmatically at every school level in the formal schooling process (a guiding vision of content and purpose).

The following ten themes serve as organizing strands for the social studies curriculum:

1. Culture
2. Time, Continuity, and Change
3. People, Places, and Environments
4. Individual Development and Identity
5. Individuals, Groups, and Institutions
6. Power, Authority, and Governance
7. Production, Distribution, and Consumption
8. Science, Technology, and Society
9. Global Connections
10. Civic Ideals and Practices

Two features of these curriculum strands are especially important. First, they are interrelated. To understand culture, for example, students need to understand time, continuity, and change; the relationships among people, places, and environments; and civic ideals and practices. To understand power, authority, and governance, students need to understand the relationships among culture; people, places, and environments; and individuals, groups, and institutions.

Second, the thematic strands draw from all of the social science disciplines and other related disciplines and fields of scholarly study to build a framework for social studies curriculum design. The ten themes thus present a holistic framework for state and local curriculum standards. To further enhance the curriculum design, social studies educators are encouraged to seek detailed content from standards developed for history, geography, civics, economics, and other fields. (See Figure A.6.)

THE VISUAL ARTS

The visual, aural, and movement arts have been prominent in human life throughout history. Before people concerned themselves with higher math or quantum physics, they were painting on cave walls and performing dances as part of religious rituals. Because human visual, auditory, and motor systems are essential to cognition, it is likely that the arts evolved to help develop and maintain these physiological systems.

In spite of this observation, numerous movements have attempted to reduce or eliminate funding for school arts. Why would a culture that values aesthetics and peak performance in the arts programs cut educational programs that prepare the next generation of artists and athletes?*

Part of the explanation lies in the current push for increased school efficiency and economy. Good arts programs may not be economically efficient. In today's world, a world obsessed with quantifying standards and students, such programs are difficult to evaluate. Educators find themselves continually having to justify arts programs, while never having to do the same for algebra or spelling. Unfortunately, justification for the arts tends to focus heavily on public performances (concerts, plays, sports, and art shows) even though such an interpretation is an extremely narrow view of what the arts represent to the human mind. The standards adopted by the National Art Education Association (NAES) are presented in Figure A.7.

---

* This discussion includes physical education and sports in the broad category of the arts.

Figure A.6   Standards for the Social Studies: The Ten Strands

---

1. CULTURE

SOCIAL STUDIES PROGRAMS SHOULD INCLUDE EXPERIENCES THAT PROVIDE FOR THE STUDY OF CULTURE AND CULTURAL DIVERSITY.

Humans create, learn, and adapt culture. Culture helps us to understand ourselves as both individuals and members of various groups. Human cultures exhibit both similarities and differences with systems of beliefs, knowledge, values, and traditions. Each system also is unique. In a democratic and multicultural society, students need to understand multiple perspectives that derive from different cultural vantage points. This understanding allows them to relate to people in our nation and throughout the world.

In schools, this theme typically appears in units and courses dealing with geography, history, and anthropology, as well as multicultural topics across the curriculum.

2. TIME, CONTINUITY, AND CHANGE

SOCIAL STUDIES PROGRAMS SHOULD INCLUDE EXPERIENCES THAT PROVIDE FOR THE STUDY OF THE WAYS HUMAN BEINGS VIEW THEMSELVES IN AND OVER TIME.

As humans, we seek to understand our historical roots and to locate ourselves in time. Such understanding involves knowing what things were like in the past and how things change and develop.

This theme typically appears in courses that:

- Include perspectives from various aspects of history
- Draw upon historical knowledge during the examination of social issues, and
- Develop the habits of mind that historians and scholars in the humanities and social sciences employ to study the past and its relationship to the present in the United States and other societies

(Continued)

Figure A.6 (Continued)

3. PEOPLE, PLACES, AND ENVIRONMENTS

SOCIAL STUDIES PROGRAMS SHOULD INCLUDE EXPERIENCES THAT PROVIDE FOR THE STUDY OF PEOPLE, PLACES, AND ENVIRONMENTS.

Technological advances connect students at all levels to the world beyond their personal locations. The study of people, places, and human-environment interactions assists learners as they create their spatial views and geographic perspectives of the world.

In schools, this theme typically appears in units and courses dealing with area studies and geography.

4. INDIVIDUAL DEVELOPMENT AND IDENTITY

SOCIAL STUDIES PROGRAMS SHOULD INCLUDE EXPERIENCES THAT PROVIDE FOR THE STUDY OF INDIVIDUAL DEVELOPMENT AND IDENTITY.

Personal identity is shaped by one's culture, by groups, and by institutional influences. Examination of various forms of human behavior enhances understanding of the relationships among social norms and emerging personal identities, the social processes that influence identity formation, and the ethical principles underlying individual action.

In schools, this theme typically appears in units and courses dealing with psychology and anthropology.

5. INDIVIDUALS, GROUPS, AND INSTITUTIONS

SOCIAL STUDIES PROGRAMS SHOULD INCLUDE EXPERIENCES THAT PROVIDE FOR THE STUDY OF INTERACTIONS AMONG INDIVIDUALS, GROUPS, AND INSTITUTIONS.

Institutions such as schools, churches, families, government agencies, and the courts all play an integral role in our lives. These and other institutions exert enormous influence over us, yet institutions are no more than organizational embodiments to further the core social values of those who comprise them. Thus, it is important that students know how institutions are formed, what controls and influences them, how they control and influence individuals and culture, and how institutions can be maintained or changed. In schools, this theme typically appears in units and courses dealing with sociology, anthropology, psychology, political science, and history.

6. POWER, AUTHORITY, AND GOVERNANCE

SOCIAL STUDIES PROGRAMS SHOULD INCLUDE EXPERIENCES THAT PROVIDE FOR THE STUDY OF HOW PEOPLE CREATE AND CHANGE STRUCTURES OF POWER, AUTHORITY, AND GOVERNANCE.

Understanding the historical development of structures of power, authority, and governance and their evolving functions in contemporary U.S. society, as well as in other parts of the world, is essential for developing civic competence.

In schools, this theme typically appears in units and courses dealing with government, politics, political science, history, law, and other social sciences.

7. PRODUCTION, DISTRIBUTION, AND CONSUMPTION

SOCIAL STUDIES PROGRAMS SHOULD INCLUDE EXPERIENCES THAT PROVIDE FOR THE STUDY OF HOW PEOPLE ORGANIZE FOR THE PRODUCTION, DISTRIBUTION, AND CONSUMPTION OF GOODS AND SERVICES.

People have wants that often exceed the limited resources available to them. As a result, a variety of ways have been invented to decide upon answers to four fundamental questions: What is to be produced? How is production to be organized? How are goods and services to be distributed? What is the most effective allocation of the factors of production (land, labor, capital, and management)? Unequal distribution of resources necessitates systems of exchange, including trade, to improve the well-being of the economy, while the role of government in economic policymaking varies over time and from place to place. Increasingly these decisions are global in scope and require systematic study of an interdependent world economy and the role of technology in economic decision making.

In schools, this theme typically appears in units and courses dealing with concepts, principles, and issues drawn from the discipline of economics.

8. SCIENCE, TECHNOLOGY, AND SOCIETY

SOCIAL STUDIES PROGRAMS SHOULD INCLUDE EXPERIENCES THAT PROVIDE FOR THE STUDY OF RELATIONSHIPS AMONG SCIENCE, TECHNOLOGY, AND SOCIETY.

Technology is as old as the first crude tool invented by prehistoric humans, but today's technology forms the basis for some of our most difficult social choices. Modern life as we know it would be impossible without technology and the science that supports it.

This theme appears in units or courses dealing with history, geography, economics, and civics and government. It draws upon several scholarly fields from the natural and physical sciences, social sciences, and the humanities for specific examples of issues from the knowledge base for considering responses to the societal issues related to science and technology.

9. GLOBAL CONNECTIONS

SOCIAL STUDIES PROGRAMS SHOULD INCLUDE EXPERIENCES THAT PROVIDE FOR THE STUDY OF GLOBAL CONNECTIONS AND INTERDEPENDENCE.

The realities of global interdependence require understanding the increasingly important and diverse global connections among world societies.

This theme typically appears in units or courses dealing with geography, culture, and economics, but again can draw upon the natural and physical sciences and the humanities, including literature, the arts, and language.

10. CIVIC IDEALS AND PRACTICES

SOCIAL STUDIES PROGRAMS SHOULD INCLUDE EXPERIENCES THAT PROVIDE FOR THE STUDY OF THE IDEALS, PRINCIPLES, AND PRACTICES OF CITIZENSHIP IN A DEMOCRATIC REPUBLIC.

An understanding of civic ideals and practices of citizenship is critical to full participation in society and is a central purpose of the social studies.

In schools, this theme typically appears in units or courses dealing with history, political science, cultural anthropology, and fields such as global studies and law-related education, while also drawing upon content from the humanities.

SOURCE: Adapted from *Standards for the Social Studies* by the National Council for the Social Studies. © 1994, by the National Council for the Social Studies.

Figure A.7   National Standards for Visual Arts Education

CONTENT STANDARDS FOR VISUAL ARTS EDUCATION

1. Understanding and applying media, techniques, and processes

2. Using knowledge of structures and functions

3. Choosing and evaluating a range of subject matter, symbols, and ideas

4. Understanding the visual arts in relation to history and cultures

5. Reflecting upon and assessing the characteristics and merits of their work and the work of others

6. Making connections between visual arts and other disciplines

SOURCE: Adapted from *National Standards for Visual Arts Education* by the National Art Education Association. Reprinted with permission from the National Art Education Association, Reston, Virginia. www.naea-reston.

Appendix II

Planning Forms

CULMINATING TASK ORGANIZER

CURRICULUM AREA(S):
GRADE LEVEL(S):
PROJECT DURATION:
RESOURCES/MATERIALS:

TASK/PROJECT DESCRIPTION

STANDARDS ADDRESSED

LANGUAGE ARTS	TECHNOLOGY
MATHEMATICS	**SCIENCE**
SOCIAL STUDIES	**VISUAL ARTS**

TASK/PROJECT OBJECTIVES

COMPREHENSION OF CONCEPTS	SKILL AND PROCESS DEVELOPMENT

PRODUCTS AND/OR PERFORMANCES

GROUP PRODUCTS	INDIVIDUAL PRODUCTS	EXTENSIONS

CRITERIA FOR TASK/PROJECT EVALUATION

GROUP PRODUCTS	INDIVIDUAL PRODUCTS	EXTENSIONS

RUBRIC ORGANIZER							
Criteria Evaluated *Specific aspects of student work to be evaluated*	**1 Novice** Beginning **No, Not Yet**	**2 Basic** Developing **Yes, But**	**3 Proficient** Accomplished **Yes**	**4 Advanced** Exemplary **Yes Plus**	**RS***	**DM**	**FS**
Criterion #1							
Criterion #2							
Criterion #3							
Criterion #4							
				Total Grade			

*RS (raw score) refers to total of all initial points achieved. Multiply raw score by difficulty multiplier (DM) for final score (FS).

RUBRIC FOR PROBLEM-BASED INSTRUCTION

Criteria Evaluated	1 Novice Beginning No, Not Yet	2 Basic Developing Yes, But	3 Proficient Accomplished Yes	4 Advanced Exemplary Yes Plus	RS*	DM	FS
					Total Grade		

*RS (raw score) refers to total of all initial points achieved. Multiply raw score by difficulty multiplier (DM) for final score (FS).

RUBRIC FOR ACCELERATED PROBLEM-BASED INSTRUCTION

Criteria Evaluated	4 Advanced Exemplary Yes Plus	3 Proficient Accomplished Yes	2 Basic Developing Yes, But	1 Novice Beginning No, Not Yet	RS*	DM	FS
				Total Grade			

*RS (raw score) refers to total of all initial points achieved. Multiply raw score by difficulty multiplier (DM) for final score (FS).

UNIT PLANNING MAP

UNIT AT A GLANCE	LESSON 1	LESSON 1 PERSPECTIVE
TOPIC: CURRICULUM AREA(S): GRADE LEVEL(S): PROJECT DURATION: UNIT OBJECTIVES:	OBJECTIVES ACTIVITIES	ENGAGING THE LEARNER: EXPLORING PRIOR KNOWLEDGE: EXPLORING NEW IDEAS/CONCEPTS: ELABORATING ON NEW LEARNING: ASSESSING STUDENT UNDERSTANDING: CLOSURE/REFLECTION:
	LESSON 2	**LESSON 2 PERSPECTIVE**
TECHNOLOGY: ASSESSMENT: RESOURCES AND MATERIALS:	OBJECTIVES ACTIVITIES	ENGAGING THE LEARNER: EXPLORING PRIOR KNOWLEDGE: EXPLORING NEW IDEAS/CONCEPTS: ELABORATING ON NEW LEARNING: ASSESSING STUDENT UNDERSTANDING: CLOSURE/REFLECTION:
	LESSON 3	**LESSON 3 PERSPECTIVE**
	OBJECTIVES ACTIVITIES	ENGAGING THE LEARNER: EXPLORING PRIOR KNOWLEDGE: EXPLORING NEW IDEAS/CONCEPTS: ELABORATING ON NEW LEARNING: ASSESSING STUDENT UNDERSTANDING: CLOSURE/REFLECTION:
	LESSON 4	**LESSON 4 PERSPECTIVE**
	OBJECTIVES ACTIVITIES	ENGAGING THE LEARNER: EXPLORING PRIOR KNOWLEDGE: EXPLORING NEW IDEAS/CONCEPTS: ELABORATING ON NEW LEARNING: ASSESSING STUDENT UNDERSTANDING: CLOSURE/REFLECTION:

UNIT OVERVIEW

UNIT AT A GLANCE
CURRICULUM AREA(S):
GRADE LEVEL(S):
UNIT GOALS AND OBJECTIVES
STUDENTS WILL . . .

RESOURCES AND MATERIALS

STANDARDS ADDRESSED

LANGUAGE ARTS	MATHEMATICS
SCIENCE	**TECHNOLOGY**
SOCIAL STUDIES	**VISUAL ARTS**
EVALUATION PLAN	**EXTENSIONS**

INTERDISCIPLINARY LESSONS

Week 1: Objectives:	Week 1 Activities
Week 2: Objectives:	Week 2 Activities
Week 3: Objectives:	Week 3 Activities
Week 4: Objectives:	Week 4 Activities

INTERDISCIPLINARY LESSON PLAN	
LESSON AT A GLANCE CURRICULUM AREA(S): GRADE LEVEL(S): LESSON DURATION: PREPARATION, RESOURCES, AND MATERIALS:	
INSTRUCTIONAL OBJECTIVES	**ONGOING ASSESSMENT**
STANDARDS ADDRESSED	
LANGUAGE ARTS	**MATHEMATICS**
SCIENCE	**TECHNOLOGY**
SOCIAL STUDIES	**VISUAL ARTS**
STEPS/PROCEDURES	
1. ENGAGING THE LEARNER	**2. EXPLORING PRIOR KNOWLEDGE**
3. EXPLORING NEW IDEAS	**4. ELABORATING ON NEW LEARNING**
5. ASSESSING STUDENT UNDERSTANDING	**6. CLOSURE AND REFLECTION**
7. METHODS FOR DIFFERENTIATION OF INSTRUCTION	**8. LESSON FOLLOW-UP AND TEACHER REFLECTION**

TEACHER'S UNIT PLAN SELF-EVALUATION RUBRIC

Criteria Evaluated	1 Novice Beginning No, Not Yet	2 Basic Developing Yes, But	3 Proficient Accomplished Yes	4 Advanced Exemplary Yes Plus	RS*	DM	FS
Unit Objectives	Objectives do not clearly describe the unit's purpose (why it is being taught).	Some of the objectives successfully describe the unit's purpose (why it is being taught) but do not place the work to come within a real-world context.	Objectives describe the unit's purpose (why it is being taught) and place the work to come within a real-world context.	Objectives target the unit's purpose (why it is being taught) and place the work to come within a highly innovative and student-oriented real-world context.		2	
Unit Planning Map or Unit Overview	Map or overview is disorganized, difficult to follow, and shows a poor understanding of the disciplines.	Map or overview shows some organization, is legible, and shows some knowledge of the disciplines.	Map or overview is organized, neat, and easy to follow, and shows an underlying understanding of the nature of the various disciplines.	Map or overview is highly concise and well written (under 2 pages), with a unique presentation that is easy to follow and demonstrates superior insight into the nature of the various disciplines.		5	
Individual Lesson Plans	Individual lesson plans do not follow the inquiry lesson model template.	There are 3 individual lesson plans, each following the inquiry lesson model template.	There are 4–5 individual lesson plans, each following the inquiry lesson model template.	There are more than 5 individual lesson plans, each closely following the inquiry lesson model template.		5	

(Continued)

	1 Novice Beginning No, Not Yet	2 Basic Developing Yes, But	3 Proficient Accomplished Yes	4 Advanced Exemplary Yes Plus			
Criteria Evaluated					RS*	DM	FS

TEACHER'S UNIT PLAN SELF-EVALUATION RUBRIC (Continued)

Criteria Evaluated	1 Novice Beginning No, Not Yet	2 Basic Developing Yes, But	3 Proficient Accomplished Yes	4 Advanced Exemplary Yes Plus	RS*	DM	FS
Hands-On Inquiry Activities	Activities or tasks are demonstrated to the class rather than experienced by the class.	Activities or tasks involve the class in some degree of active learning.	Activities or tasks involve the entire class in active, meaningful, and relevant learning.	Creative and unusual activities or tasks involve the entire class in active, meaningful, and relevant learning.		1	
Unit Integration	Subject areas are not integrated well.	2 subject areas are successfully integrated.	3 different subject areas are successfully integrated.	More than 3 different subject areas are successfully integrated.		2	
Culminating Task Organizer	Organizer is incomplete and does not fully describe all criteria.	Organizer is complete but does not fully describe all criteria.	Organizer is complete and fully describes all criteria.	Organizer is comprehensive, is well written, and fully describes all criteria.		5	
Assessment Plan	• Plan contains 1 rubric, but that rubric is not consistently valid. • Plan does not promote student reflection.	• Plan contains 1 well-designed rubric that validly assesses the unit. • Plan contains only 1 opportunity for student reflection.	• Plan contains more than 1 comprehensive rubric that provides ongoing and valid assessment. • Plan contains several opportunities for student reflection.	• Plan contains several rubrics that assess the work throughout the unit with a high degree of validity. • Plan contains numerous and varied opportunities for student reflection.		5	
				Total Grade			

Bibliography

Andrade, H. (2000). Using rubrics to promote thinking and learning. *Educational Leadership, 57*(5), 13–18. (Original published 1994)

Armstrong, T. (2000). *Multiple intelligences in the classroom* (2nd ed.). Alexandria, VA: Association for Supervision and Curriculum Development.

Barell, J. (1997). *Problem-based learning: An inquiry approach.* Thousand Oaks, CA: Corwin Press.

Battista, T. (1999). The mathematical miseducation of America's youth: Ignoring research and scientific study in education. *Phi Delta Kappan, 80*(6), 424–433.

Bellanca, J., Chapman, C., & Swartz, E. (1997). *Multiple assessments for multiple intelligences* (3rd ed.). Thousand Oaks, CA: Corwin Press.

Blum, R. E., & Arter, J. A. (Eds.). (1996). *A handbook for student performance assessment in an era of restructuring.* Alexandria, VA: Association for Supervision and Curriculum Development.

Bredekamp, S., & Copple, C. (Eds.). (1997). *Developmentally appropriate practice in early childhood programs.* Washington, DC: National Association for the Education of Young Children.

Brooks, J., & Brooks, M. (1999). *In search of understanding: The case for constructivist classrooms.* Alexandria, VA: Association for Supervision and Curriculum Development.

Bruer, T. (1998). Brain science, brain fiction. *Educational Leadership, 56*(3), 14–18.

Burke, K. (1997). *How to assess authentic learning.* Thousand Oaks, CA: Corwin Press.

Caine, G., & Caine, R. N. (1994). *Making connections: Teaching and the human brain.* Menlo Park, CA: Addison-Wesley.

Caine, G., & Caine, R. N. (1997a). *Education on the edge of possibility.* Alexandria, VA: Association for Supervision and Curriculum Development.

Caine, G., & Caine, R. N. (1997b). *Unleashing the power of perceptual change: The potential of brain-based teaching.* Alexandria, VA: Association for Supervision and Curriculum Development.

Caine, G., & Caine, R. N. (1999). *MindShifts: A brain-compatible process for professional development and the renewal of education* (2nd ed.). Tucson, AZ: Zephyr.

Caine, G., Caine, R., & McClintic, C. (2002). Guiding the innate constructivist. *Educational Leadership, 60*(1), 70–73.

Carr, J., & Harris, D. (2001). *Succeeding with standards: Linking curriculum, assessment, and action planning.* Alexandria, VA: Association for Supervision and Curriculum Development.

Cole, R. (1997). *Educating everybody's children: Diverse teaching strategies for diverse learners.* Alexandria, VA: Association for Supervision and Curriculum Development.

Costa, A., & Kallick, B. (2000a). *Activating and engaging habits of mind.* Alexandria, VA: Association for Supervision and Curriculum Development.

Costa, A., & Kallick, B. (2000b). *Discovering and exploring habits of mind.* Alexandria, VA: Association for Supervision and Curriculum Development.

Danielson, C. (1996). *Enhancing professional practice: A framework for teaching.* Alexandria, VA: Association for Supervision and Curriculum Development.

D'Arcangelo, M. (1998). The brains behind the brain. *Educational Leadership, 56*(3), 20–25.

Davis, J. (1997). *Mapping the mind: The secrets of the human brain and how it works.* Secaucus, NJ: Carol Publishing Group.

Dehaene, S. (1997). *The number sense: How the mind creates mathematics.* New York: Oxford University Press.

Dehaene, S. (2001). *The cognitive neuroscience of consciousness.* London: MIT Press.

Delisle, R. (1997). *How to use problem-based learning in the classroom.* Alexandria, VA: Association for Supervision and Curriculum Development.

Dewey, J. (1902). *The child and the curriculum.* Chicago: University of Chicago Press.

Dewey, J. (1938). *Experience and education.* New York: Macmillan.

Diamond, M., & Hopson, J. (1998). *Magic trees of the mind: How to nurture your child's intelligence, creativity, and healthy emotions from birth through adolescence.* New York: Dutton.

Drake, S. (1998). *Creating integrated curriculum: Proven ways to increase student learning.* Thousand Oaks, CA: Corwin Press.

Edelman, G. (1987). *Neural Darwinism: The theory of neuronal group selection.* New York: Basic Books.

Education Week. (2001). *Quality counts 2001—A better balance: Standards, tests, and the tools to succeed.* Bethesda, MD: Editorial Projects in Education.

Education Week/Pew Charitable Trusts. (1997). *Quality counts: A report card on the condition of public education in the 50 states.* Bethesda, MD: Editorial Projects in Education.

Educators in Connecticut's Pomperaug Regional School District 15. (1996). *A teacher's guide to performance-based learning and assessment.* Alexandria, VA: Association for Supervision and Curriculum Development.

Elman, J., Bates, E., Johnson, M., Karmiloff-Smith, A., Parisi, D., & Plunkett, K. (1998). *Rethinking innateness.* Cambridge, MA: MIT Press.

Erickson, L. (1998). *Concept-based curriculum and instruction.* Thousand Oaks, CA: Corwin Press.

Felner, R. D. (1995). The process and impact of school reform and restructuring for the middle years: A longitudinal study of turning points–based comprehensive school change. In R. Takaniski & D. Hamburg (Eds.), *Frontiers in the education of young adolescents.* New York: Carnegie Corporation.

Fischer, C. F., & King, R. M. (1995). *Authentic assessment: A guide to implementation.* Thousand Oaks, CA: Corwin Press.

Fisher, D., & Roach, V. (1999). *Opening doors: Connecting students to curriculum, classmates, and learning.* Colorado Springs, CO: PEAK Parent Center.

Foster, M., & Masters, G. (1996). *Portfolio assessment resource kit.* Camberwell, Victoria, Australia: Australian Council for Educational Research.

Freedman, R. (1994). *Open-ended questioning: A handbook for educators.* Menlo Park, CA: Addison-Wesley.

Gardner, H. (1983). *Frames of mind.* New York: Basic Books.

Gardner, H. (1987). Beyond IQ: Education and human development. *Harvard Educational Review, 57*(2), 187–193.

Gardner, H. (1993a). *Creating minds.* New York: Basic Books.

Gardner, H. (1993b). *Multiple intelligences: The theory in practice.* New York: Basic Books.

Gardner, H. (1999). *The disciplined mind: What all students should understand.* New York: Simon and Schuster.

Gardner, H. (2005). *Multiple lenses on the mind.* Paper presented at the ExpoGestion Conference. Bogota, Colombia, May 25, 2005.

Goleman, D. (1995). *Emotional intelligence: Why it can matter more than IQ.* New York: Bantam Books.

Gronlund, N. (2000). *How to write and use instructional objectives* (6th ed.). Upper Saddle River, NJ: Merrill.

Guskey, T. (1996). Reporting on student learning: Lessons from the past—prescriptions for the future. In T. Guskey (Ed.), *Communicating student learning: 1996 yearbook of the Association for Supervision and Curriculum Development.* Alexandria, VA: Association for Supervision and Curriculum Development.

Haladyna, T. (1999). *A complete guide to student grading.* Boston, MA: Allyn & Bacon.

Hart, D. (1994). *Authentic assessment: A handbook for educators.* Menlo Park, CA: Addison-Wesley.

Hart, L. (1998). *Human brain and human learning* (2nd ed.). Kent, WA: Books for Educators.

Hill, B., & Ruptic, C. (1994). *Practical aspects of authentic assessment: Putting the pieces together.* Norwood, MA: Christopher-Gordon.

Hymes, D. L., Chafin, A. E., & Gondor, P. (1991). *The changing face of testing and assessment: Problems and solutions.* Arlington, VA: American Association of School Administrators.

Illinois State Board of Education. (1995). *Effective scoring rubrics—A guide to their development and use.* Springfield: Illinois Board of Education.

International Reading Association and the National Association for the Education of Young Children. (1998). *Official position statement.* Washington, DC: National Association for the Education of Young Children.

International Society for Technology in Education. (2000). *National educational technology standards for students: Connecting curriculum and technology.* Eugene, OR: Author.

Jensen, E. (1998). *Teaching with the brain in mind.* Alexandria, VA: Association for Supervision and Curriculum Development.

Jensen, E. (2005). *Teaching with the brain in mind* (2nd ed.). Alexandria, VA: Association of Supervision and Curriculum Development.

Johnson, D., Johnson, R., & Holubec, E. (1994). *The new circles of learning: Cooperation in the classroom and school.* Alexandria, VA: Association for Supervision and Curriculum Development.

Kendall, J., & Marzano, R. (1995). *The systematic identification and articulation on content standards and benchmarks: Update.* Aurora, CO: McREL.

Kessler, R. (2000). *The soul of education.* Alexandria, VA: Association for Supervision and Curriculum Development.

Kotulak, R. (1996). *Inside the brain: Revolutionary discoveries of how the mind works.* Kansas City, MO: Andrews & McMeel.

Kovalik, S. (1995). *Integrated thematic instruction: The model.* Kent, WA: Books for Educators.

Kovalik, S., & Olsen, K. (1997). *ITI: The model—Integrated thematic instruction* (3rd ed.). Kent, WA: Susan Kovalik & Associates.

Krumboltz, J., & Yeh, C. (1996). Competitive grading sabotages good teaching. *Phi Delta Kappan, 78*(4), 324–326.

Lake, R., Hill, P., O'Toole, L., & Celio, M. (1999). *Making standards work: Active voices, focused learning.* Seattle, WA: Center on Reinventing Public Education.

Lambdin, D., Kehle, P., & Preston, R. (Eds.). (1996). *Emphasis on assessment: Readings from the NCTM's school-based journals.* Reston, VA: National Council of Teachers of Mathematics.

Latham, A. (1997). Learning through feedback. *Educational Leadership, 54*(8), 86–87.

Lazear, D. 1994. *Multiple intelligence approaches to assessment: Solving the assessment conundrum.* Tucson, AZ: Zephyr.

LeDoux, J. (1996). *The emotional brain: The mysterious underpinnings of emotional life.* New York: Simon and Schuster.

Lopez-Reyna, N., & Bay, M. (1997). Enriching assessment: Using varied assessments for diverse learners. *Teaching Exceptional Children, 29*(4), 33–37.

Lustig, K. (1996). *Portfolio assessment: A handbook for middle level educators.* Columbus, OH: National Middle School Association.

Mandel, S. (1998). *Social studies in the cyberage.* Arlington Heights, IL: SkyLight Training and Publishing.

Mangan, M. A. (1998). *Brain-compatible science.* Thousand Oaks, CA: Corwin Press.

Marzano, R. (1999). Building curriculum and assessments around standards. *High School Magazine, 6*(5), 14–19.

Marzano, R. (2000). *Transforming classroom grading.* Alexandria, VA: Association for Supervision and Curriculum Development.

Mason, J., & Sinha, S. (1993). Emerging literacy in the early childhood years: Applying a Vygotskian model of learning and development. In B. Spodek (Ed.), *Handbook of research on the education of young children* (pp. 137–150). New York: Macmillan.

McTighe, J. (1994). *Developing performance assessment tasks: A resource guide.* Frederick County: Maryland Assessment Consortium.

Mosle, S. (1996, October 27). The answer is national standards. *New York Times Magazine,* pp. 45–47, 56, 68.

Nagel, N. (1996). *Learning through real-world problem solving: The power of integrative teaching.* Thousand Oaks, CA: Corwin Press.

National Academy of Sciences. (1996). *National science education standards.* Washington, DC: National Academy Press.

National Art Education Association. (1994). *National standards for visual arts education.* Reston, VA: Author.

National Center for Education Statistics, Office of Educational Research and Improvement. (1996). *Pursuing excellence: A study of curriculum and achievement in international context.* Washington, DC: U.S. Department of Education.

National Council for the Social Studies. (1994). *Expectations of excellence: Curriculum standards for social studies.* Waldort, MD Author.

National Council of Teachers of Mathematics. (2000). *Principles and standards for school mathematics.* Reston, VA: Author.

National Research Council. (2000). *How people learn: Brain, mind, experience, and school.* Washington, DC: National Academy Press.

National Research Council. (2002). *A sampler of national science education standards.* Upper Saddle River, NJ: Merrill.

O'Brien, T. C. (1999). Parrot math. *Phi Delta Kappan, 80*(6), 434–438.

Ogle, D. (1986). K-W-L group instruction strategy. In A. Palincsar, D. Ogle, B. Jones, & E. Carr (Eds.). *Teaching reading as thinking.* Alexandria, VA: Association for Supervision and Curriculum Development.

Pate, P., Homestead, E., & McGinnis, K. (1997). *Making integrated curriculum work: Teachers, students, and the quest for coherent curriculum.* New York: Teachers College Press.

Pike, K., & Salend, S. (1995). Authentic assessment strategies: Alternatives to norm-referenced testing. *Teaching Exceptional Students, 28*(1), 15–20.

Pinker, S. (1997). *How the mind works.* New York: Norton.

Religeluth, C. (1997). Educational standards: To standardize or customize learning? *Phi Delta Kappan, 79,* 202–206.

Riley, J. (1996). *The teaching of reading.* London: Paul Chapman.

Roblyer, M. D., & Edwards, J. (2000). *Integrating educational technology into teaching* (2nd ed.). Upper Saddle River, NJ: Merrill.

Rodman, B., & Lindsay, D. (Eds.). (1997, February). Quality counts: A special report. *Teacher Magazine.* Editorial Projects in Education, 19–55.

Ronis, D. (2007a). *Brain-compatible assessment.* Thousand Oaks, CA: Corwin Press.

Ronis, D. (2007b). *Brain-compatible mathematics.* Thousand Oaks, CA: Corwin Press.

Ronis, D. (2007c). *PBL: Problem-based learning for math and science: Integrating inquiry and the Internet.* Thousand Oaks, CA: Corwin Press.

Sereno, M. I. (1991a). Four analogies between biological and cultural/linguistic evolution. *Journal of Theoretical Biology, 151,* 467–507.

Sereno, M. I. (1991b). *Language and the primate brain.* Proceedings, Thirteenth Annual Conference of the Cognitive Science Society, Lawrence Erlbaum Association, 79–84.

Sereno, M. I. (1999). Brain mapping in animals and humans. *Current Opinion in Neurobiology, 8,* 188–194.

Sereno, M. I. (2005). Language origins without the semantic urge. *Cognitive Science Online, 3,* 1–12.

Silver, H., Strong, R., & Perini, M. (2000). *So each may learn: Integrating learning styles and multiple intelligences.* Alexandria, VA: Association for Supervision and Curriculum Development.

Simon, H. A. (1996). *Models of my life* (3rd ed.). Cambridge, MA: MIT Press.

Sirotnik, K. A., & Kimball, K. (1999). Standards for standards-based accountability systems. *Phi Delta Kappan, 81*(3), 209–214.

Snow, C., Burns, M. S., & Griffin, P. (1998). *Preventing reading difficulties in young children.* Washington, DC: National Academy Press.

Sousa, D. (1998). *Learning manual for how the brain learns.* Thousand Oaks, CA: Corwin Press.

Sprenger, M. (1999). *Learning and memory: The brain in action.* Alexandria, VA: Association for Supervision and Curriculum Development.

St. George, M., Kutas, M., Martinez, A., & Sereno, M. I. (1999). Semantic integration in reading: Engagement of the right hemisphere during discourse processing. *Brain, 122,* 1317–1325.

Sternberg, R. (1996). *Successful intelligence: How practical and creative intelligence determine success in life.* New York: Simon and Schuster.

Sternberg, R. (1999a). Successful intelligence: Finding a balance. *Trends in Cognitive Sciences, 3,* 436–442.

Sternberg, R. (1999b). The theory of successful intelligence. *Review of General Psychology, 3,* 292–316.

Sternberg, R., Forsythe, G., Hedlund, J., Horvath, J., Snook, S., Williams, W., et al. (2000). *Practical intelligence.* New York: Cambridge University Press.

Stiggins, R. (1994). *Student-centered classroom assessment.* New York: Macmillan.

Stiggins, R. (2001). *Student-involved classroom assessment* (3rd ed.). Upper Saddle River, NJ: Merrill.

Strong, R., Silver, H., & Perini, M. (2001). *Teaching what matters most: Standards and strategies for raising student achievement.* Alexandria, VA: Association for Supervision and Curriculum Development.

Sylwester, R. (1995). *A celebration of neurons: An educator's guide to the human brain.* Alexandria, VA: Association for Supervision and Curriculum Development.

Sylwester, R. (2000). *A biological brain in a cultural classroom.* Thousand Oaks, CA: Corwin Press.

Taggart, G., & Wilson, W. (1998). *Promoting reflective thinking in teachers.* Thousand Oaks, CA: Corwin Press.

Treadwell, M. (2001). *1001 of the best Internet sites for educators.* Thousand Oaks, CA: Corwin Press.

Valverde, G., & Schmidt, W. (1997/1998, Winter). Refocusing U.S. math and science education. *Issues in Science and Technology,* pp. 60–66.

Vars, G. F. (1997). Student concerns and standards too. *Middle School Journal, 28,* 44–49.

Westwater, A., & Wolfe, P. (2000). The brain-compatible curriculum. *Educational Leadership, 58*(3), 49–52.

Wiggins, G., & McTighe, J. (1998). *Understanding by design.* Alexandria, VA: Association for Supervision and Curriculum Development.

Williams, R. B., & Dunn, S. E. (2007). *Brain-compatible learning for the block.* Thousand Oaks, CA: Corwin Press.

Willoughby, S. S. (1996). The standards: Some second thoughts. *Mathematics Teaching in the Middle School, 2*(1), 8–11.

Winograd, P., & Perkins, F. (1998). Revisiting effective teaching. *Educational Leadership 56*(3), 61–64.

Wolfe, P. (2001). *Brain matters: Translating research into classroom practice.* Alexandria, VA: Association for Supervision and Curriculum Development.

Wood, K., McCormack, R., Lapp, D., & Flood, J. (1997, January). Improving young adolescents' literacy through collaborative learning. *Middle School Journal,* pp. 26–33.

Index

Accountability, vii, viii
Acquisition of information, vii
Active learning, xi, xii, 24, 68–69,
    69 (figure), 110
Administrators, vii
Advanced assessment rubric, 50–51
Alternative assessments, 39
Ancient Egypt lesson, 52–57
Arts instruction. *See* Visual arts
    instruction
Assessment, vii
  alternative/authentic
    assessment, 39, 73
  interdisciplinary performance
    assessments, 39
  meaningful learning and, viii–ix
  quality assessment, characteristics of,
    40, 40 (figure)
  student understanding, 93
  See also Performance assessment
    models; Teacher self-evaluation;
    Unit assessment plan
Attention, 24–25
Authentic assessment, 39, 73
Authentic problem-solving, vi–xii,
    27 (figure)

Backward design format, 3
Barell, J., 91
Best practices, 73, 93
Brain function, viii, 23–24
  brain growth/development,
    26 (figure)
  emotions and, 24–25
  learning process and, xi–xii, 23–25,
    24 (figure), 26 (figure)
  social interaction and, 25

Caine, G., 24
Caine, R. N., 24
Case studies, 68
Center for Education Reform, 104
Centralized education reform, vii
Clustering content areas, 70, 70 (figure)
Collaborative learning, xii
Competitive environments, 25
Complex problems, xii, 2, 93–94
Comprehension, vii, 23
Constructivist perspective, xi, xii
Content area standards, 2, 28
  instructional principles, 108–110
  language arts, 45–46, 116,
    117 (figure)
  mathematics, 46–48, 105–110,
    106–108 (figures)
  science, 110, 111–114 (figure)
  social studies, 84–85, 116–118,
    119–121 (figure)
  state-level standards, 103–104
  visual arts, 118–119, 121 (figure)
  See also Unit overview; Unit
    planning maps
Content knowledge, viii, xi–xii
  clustering content areas, 70,
    70 (figure)
  student perspective on, 28, 44, 46
  See also Content area standards;
    Knowledge
Conventional teaching, xi–xii
Council of Chief State School
    Officers, 104
Creativity, xii
Culminating task organizers, 3–4
  ancient Egypt lesson, 52–53
  earthquakes lesson, 18–19

form for, 124
human body travel lesson, 58–59
meaningful learning, design of,
    25–28, 27–28 (figures)
money, money, money lesson, 14–15
theme park lesson, 29–30
trip to outer space lesson, 78–80
weathering the storm lesson, 95–96
write your own textbook
    lesson, 36–37
Culminating task rubrics, 3, 5
ancient Egypt lesson, 54–55
form for, 125
money, money, money lesson, 15
theme park lesson, 31
trip to outer space lesson, 81–83
Cultural structures, viii
Curriculum development, ix, 67–68
case studies, 68
curricular models and, 68–70
integrated instruction and, 2–3
problem-based learning and, 68–69
service learning and, 69
standards and, 1–2
thematic learning, 70, 70 (figure)
See also Content area standards;
    Instruction; Interdisciplinary unit
    plan; Meaningful learning;
    Standards; Unit planning
Curriculum and Evaluation
    Standards, 105

Deep understanding, vii, 23
Dehaene, S., 24
Design rubric, 31
active learner inquiry and,
    68, 69 (figure)
integrated instruction and,
    3, 3 (figure), 6
planning for meaning and, 67
unit change/development and, 67–68
See also Unit overview;
    Unit planning maps
Difficulty multiplier (DM), 41–42
Dunn, S. E., 70

Earthquakes lesson, 18–22
Education reform, vii, 1–2, 104
Elaborating on learning, 92–93
Emotional investment, xi,
    24–25, 26 (figure)

Engaged learners, 92
Equity ethic, 108
Evaluation. *See* Assessment; Teacher
    self-evaluation; Unit assessment plan
Experience-based learning, vii–viii, xi–xiii

Facilitator role, 24
Family structures, viii
Final score (FS), 42
Forms. *See* Planning forms
Forsythe, G., 24

Gardner, H., 24
Globalization, vii
Goleman, D., 24
Group work rubric, 61–62

Hedlund, J., 24
Horvath, J., 24
Human body travel lesson, 58–65

Inclusive classrooms, 51
Individual Education Plan (IEP), 41
Individual work rubric, 60
Inductive format, xii
Information acquisition
    model, vii, xi, xii
Inquiry-based learning, xi–xii, 2, 68–69
Instruction:
    integrated/interdisciplinary
        instruction, xi–xii
    lesson plans, foundation of, 93
    See also Curriculum development;
        Interdisciplinary unit plan;
        Learning; Meaningful learning;
        Standards; Unit assessment plan;
        Unit planning
Integrated instruction, xi–xii, xiii
    brain function and, 24, 24 (figure)
    design tools for, 3, 3 (figure), 6
    knowledge, evolution of, 1
    standards and, 2–3
    See also Interdisciplinary unit plan;
        Standards; Unit planning
Interactive environments, xi,
    25, 26 (figure)
Interdisciplinary performance
    assessments, 39
    scoring rubric, 40–42
    See also Performance assessment
        models; Unit assessment plan

Interdisciplinary unit plan, xii–xiii, 91
  complex problems and, 93–94
  design process and, xiii, 6, 67–68,
    69 (figure)
  elaborating on learning and, 92–93
  engaged learners and, 92
  environmental/contextual
    elements and, 94
  example lesson, 95–101
  form for, 130
  fundamental instructional
    strategies and, 93
  idea exploration and, 92
  prior knowledge and, 92
  template for, 10, 11–12
  unit planning map, lesson
    perspective section of, 91–93
  See also Content area standards;
    Standards; Unit overview; Unit
    planning; Unit planning maps
International Reading Association (IRA),
    2, 42, 45–46, 116, 117 (figure)
International Society for Technology
    in Education (ISTE), 2, 110, 115,
    115 (figure)
Internet resources, vii, 71, 72 (figure)
  professional organization sites, 104
  state-level content standards,
    103–104

Jensen, E., 24
Journal rubric, 33

Knowledge, vii, viii
  content knowledge, viii, xi–xii
  evolution of, 1
  inquiry-based learning and, xi–xii
  prior knowledge, xii-xiii, 2, 26, 73, 92
  surface knowledge, 23
  transfer of, 2, 73
  See also Instruction; Learning;
    Unit planning

Language arts instruction, 45–46,
    70 (figure), 116, 117 (figure)
Learning:
  acquisition model of, vii
  brain function and, xi–xii, 24,
    24 (figure)
  collaborative approach to, xii
  comprehension and, vii
  conventional vs. constructivist
    perspective on, xi–xii
  emotional investment and, xi
  experiential learning, vii–viii, xi–xii
  prior knowledge and, xii–xiii
  self-motivated learning, xi
  social/cultural influences on, viii
  social interaction and, xi
  student-centered vs.
    teacher-centered, xi–xii
  See also Assessment; Meaningful
    learning; Instruction; Standards;
    Teaching; Unit planning
Lesson models, 3
Lesson perspective section,
    73, 91–93
Lesson planning. *See* Interdisciplinary
    unit plan; Unit overview; Unit
    planning; Unit planning maps
Lived experience, vii–viii, xi–xiii

Map rubric, 32
  See also Unit planning maps
Mathematics instruction, 46–48,
    70 (figure), 105–110,
    106–108 (figures)
McClintic, C., 24
Meaningful learning, 23
  assessment and, viii–ix
  authentic problems and, xi, xii
  brain function and, 23–24,
    24 (figure), 26 (figure)
  constructivist approach and, xi–xii
  culminating task organization,
    25–28, 27–28 (figures)
  emotional investment
    and, xi, 24–25
  example lessons, 29–38
  social interaction and, xi, 25
  student perspective, content
    valuation and, 28
  surface knowledge and, 23
  See also Instruction;
    Interdisciplinary unit plan;
    Learning; Unit planning
Metacognition, 73, 92
Money, money, money lesson, 14–17
Motivation. *See* Self-motivated
    learning
Multisensory involvement, 26 (figure)
Music instruction, 70 (figure)

National Academy of Sciences (NAS), 2, 110
National Art Education Association (NAES), 119, 121 (figure)
National Council for the Social Studies (NCSS), 2, 84–85, 116–118, 119–121 (figure)
National Council of Teachers of English (NCTE), 2, 42, 45–46, 116, 117 (figure)
National Council of Teachers of Mathematics (NCTM), 2, 42, 46–48, 105–110
National Educational Technology Standards for Students: Connecting Curriculum and Technology, 115
National Science Education Standards (NSES), 110, 111–114 (figure)
Neuroscience. *See* Brain function

Objective evaluation, 39–40
Observation, 39
Open-ended problems, xii

Parents. *See* Family structures
Performance assessment models, 39–40
  progress assessment rubric and, 42–44
  scoring rubric and, 40–42
  See also Assessment; Rubrics; Unit assessment plan
Physical education instruction, 70 (figure)
Planning forms:
  accelerated problem-based instruction, 127
  culminating task organizer, 124
  interdisciplinary unit plan, 130
  problem-based instruction, 126
  rubric organizer, 125
  teacher self-evaluation rubric, 131–132
  unit overview, 129
  unit planning map, 128
Political policy, vii, viii
Portfolios, 39
Principles and Standards for School Mathematics, 105–110, 107–108 (figure)

Prior knowledge, xii–xiii, 2, 26, 73, 92
Problem-based learning (PBL), xi–xii, 2, 25
  form for, 126
  language arts and, 116
  problem-based instruction rubric, 49–50, 68–69, 126–127
  solution-based learning and, xi
  technology and, 115
Production-line model of learning, vii
Professional development, 93
Professional organizations, 104
Progress assessment rubric, 42–44
Project approach to learning, xi–xii

Quality assessment, 40, 40 (figure)

Raw score (RS), 42
Readiness, 26
Real-world problems, xi–xii, 2, 23, 25, 39
Reflection, 92, 93
Reform movement in education, vii, 1–2, 104
Research-based practice, viii, 24
  See also Rubrics; Standards
Ronis, D., 24, 124–132
Rote learning, vii, xii, 1, 23, 24
Rubrics, 5
  advanced assessment rubric, 50–51
  culminating task rubric, 3, 5
  design methodology, 41–42, 42–43 (figures)
  design rubric, 31, 67–68, 69 (figure)
  group work rubric, 61–62
  inclusion classrooms, assessment rubric for, 51
  individual work rubric, 60
  journal rubric, 33
  language arts rubric, 45–46
  map rubric, 32
  problem-based instruction rubric, 49–50, 126
  progress assessment rubric, 42–44
  scoring rubric, 40–42
  standards/goals communication and, 40–41
  student-designed rubrics, 44, 46

teacher self-evaluation rubric, 10, 12–14, 131–132
See also Standards; Unit assessment plan; Unit overview; Unit planning; Unit planning maps

Science instruction, 70 (figure), 110, 111–114 (figure)
Scoring rubric, 40–42
final score, 42
raw score, 42
See also Unit assessment plan
Self-evaluation. *See* Teacher self-evaluation rubric
Self-gratification philosophy, viii
Self-motivated learning, xi, 25
Sereno, M. I., 24
Service learning, 69
Simon, H. A., 1
Snook, S., 24
Social interaction, xi, 25, 26 (figure)
Social structures, viii
Social studies instruction, 70 (figure), 84–85, 116–118, 119–121 (figure)
Socialization, 25
Solution-based learning, xi
Standards, 1–2
curricular models and, 68–70, 70 (figure)
integrated instruction and, 2–3
professional organizations for, 104
scoring rubric and, 40–42
state-level standards, 103–104
unit planning and, 2
See also Content area standards; Rubrics; Unit assessment plan
State-level content standards, 103–104
Sternberg, R., 24
Student-centered learning, xi–xii, 24
Student-designed rubrics, 44, 46
Student perspective on content, 28
Surface knowledge, 23

Tasks. *See* Culminating task organizers; Culminating task rubrics
Teacher self-evaluation, 10, 12–14, 93, 131–132
See also Rubrics; Unit assessment plan

Teaching, viii
constructivist approach to, xi, xii
conventional teaching, xi–xii
facilitator role and, 24
inductive format and, xii
integrated lesson design and, 24
interdisciplinary unit planning and, xii–xiii
self-evaluation rubric, 10, 12–14, 93, 131–132
standards, role of, 1–2
teacher-centered approach to, xi–xii, 24
See also Instruction; Learning; Standards; Unit planning
Technology, vii, 71
mathematics instruction and, 109–110
standards for, 110, 115, 115 (figure)
See also Internet resources
Testing. *See* Assessment
Thematic learning, 70, 70 (figure)
Theme park lesson, 29–35
Transfer of knowledge, 2, 73
Trip to outer space lesson, 78–89

Understanding, vii, 23, 93
Unit assessment plan:
advanced assessment rubric, 50–51
descriptor levels and, 42–43
design methodology and, 41–42, 41–43 (figures)
difficulty multiplier and, 41–42
example lessons, 52–65
inclusive classrooms, assessment rubric for, 51
language arts rubric, 45–46
mathematics rubric, 46–48
performance assessment and, 39–40
problem-based instruction rubric, 49–50
progress assessment rubric, 42–44
quality assessment, characteristics of, 40, 40 (figure)
scoring rubrics and, 40–42
student-designed rubrics and, 44, 46
See also Unit overview; Unit planning maps

Unit overview, 6, 9–10, 73,
76–77 (figure)
ancient Egypt lesson, 56–57
curricular models and, 68–70,
70 (figure)
form for, 129
resources/materials and, 71–72,
72 (figure)
selection criteria, 70–71, 71 (figure)
trip to outer space lesson, 78–89
unit design and, 67–68, 69 (figure)
See also Interdisciplinary unit plan; Unit
planning; Unit planning maps
Unit planning, xii–xiii
backward design format and, 3
culminating task organizer, 3–4,
14–15, 18–19
culminating task rubrics, 5, 15
examples of, 14–22
integrated instruction and, 2–3,
3 (figure), 6
interdisciplinary lesson plan, 10, 11–12
knowledge, evolution of, 1
standards, role of, 1–3
teacher self-evaluation rubric, 10, 12–14
unit overview, 6, 9–10
unit planning maps, 3, 6, 7–8
See also Meaningful learning; Planning
forms; Rubrics; Standards; Unit
assessment plan; Unit overview;
Unit planning maps

Unit planning maps, 3, 6, 7–8, 72–73,
74–75 (figure)
curricular models and, 68–70,
70 (figure)
earthquakes lesson, 20–22
form for, 128
human body travel lesson, 63–65
lesson perspective section of, 73,
91–93
money, money, money
lesson, 16–17
resources/materials and, 71–72,
72 (figure)
selection criteria, 70–71, 71 (figure)
theme park lesson, 34–35
unit design and, 67–68, 69 (figure)
weathering the storm lesson, 98–100
See also Interdisciplinary unit plan;
Unit assessment plan; Unit
overview; Unit planning

Visual arts instruction, 70 (figure),
118–119, 121 (figure)

Weathering the storm lesson, 95–101
Web resources. *See* Internet resources
Williams, R. B., 70
Williams, W., 24
Wisdom, vii
Wolfe, P., 24
Write your own textbook lesson, 36–38